Seamus Heaney and the Great Poetry Hoax

A critical exposé of Faber and Faber's verse-man

By Kevin Kiely

D1465348

books by the author:

Quintesse (St Martin's Press)

Mere Mortals (Poolbeg)

A Horse Called El Dorado (O'Brien Press)

SOS Lusitania (O'Brien Press)

Francis Stuart: Artist and Outcast (Liffey Press/Areopagitica)

Breakfast with Sylvia (Lagan Press)

Plainchant for a Sundering (Lapwing Press)

The Welkinn Complex (Number One Son Publishing, Co., Florida)

UCD Belfield Metaphysical: A Retrospective (Lapwing Press)

UCD Belfield Metaphysical: New and Selected Poems
(Areopagitica)

Harvard's Patron: Jack of all Poets (Areopagitica)

CONTENTS

Mary de Rachewiltz (Ezra Pound's daughter), Seamus Heaney and
Kevin Kiely in Trinity College Dublin, (July) 2013

Introduction: Heaney's travesty of rural life

'Frost was at home in the high cultural context of the university courses, but he still gave you a link back down into what you stored in your own intimate child-body, the tramping of hay.   So I responded immediately to that primal reach into the physical'

—Stepping Stones

I told me brother Seamus

I'll go off and get right famous

And when I come back home again

I'll have seen the whole wide world

Goodbye, Muirshin Durkin

I'm sick and tired of workin'

I'll no more dig the praties

No more be a fool

—Nineteenth Century Ballad

I admit from the outset that my case contra Heaney (hereafter H), is not *ad hominem*, or to his individual being, such as it was, and the case is made by close reading, analysis, and minutely examining his verse, and less so his critical output which is reflected in the opening quote. H emerged through the 'media-poetry scene' which is the subtext of the critical analysis that follows.

Critical writing is never offensive or shabby: it is about quality, ethics, and the expert appraisal of poetry, prose and other verbal art forms. It is a discipline inherent in writing poetry and prose to their final form, and that is from where I hail. I have had to ingest some guile and wit into the book because the grim turgidity of H's verse resonates at a low threshold that can barely enliven the discussion. H's verse product evokes shock because of its shallow provenance, and begs to be exposed as a gross infamy. The whole pretence of H posturing as literature-maker began when I was immediately repulsed on first sighting his verse which is related later.

H's use of 'high cultural context' and 'the tramping of hay' (above) with his mention of 'intimate child-body' and 'the physical' redolently locates him as I will show: the fake farm-boy serving the cash-cow of the campus and the media poetry scene during a time of sectarian war in Ireland.

H's Wordsworthian pretensions are far too irritating to demand much unravelling. Frost's poems cover the material which H largely re-uses, as in the rural anecdotes and dialogue-verse. H is, of course, a miniature Frost in verse; doesn't have any wit and whimsy which Frost purveyed, but H certainly absorbed the melodrama of being out there in the countryside and 'sold' it to a gullible, complicit academic audience, if less so to the cognoscenti of poetry. It will be offensive to some that there even exist cognoscenti of poetry, but you can hardly have expected the art form to have survived for centuries through verse-making cliques, 'poetry-careerists' and the likes of H.

Frost's *North of Boston* gave H his title *North*. All of Frost's work in *North of Boston* (1914) *Mountain Interval* (1916) and *New Hampshire* (1923) meant that H's rural nostalgia is redundant: the ground was already covered (no pun intended). H's verse is a subconscious homage to Frost, except that H's retro is not as good as Frost at his 'best'. There is no need for H. Frost's verse has already done the rural themes which H pilfered. Frost is sufficient in this rank but I am not much into Frost either.

In Ireland, we had Patrick Kavanagh, a poet who abandoned rural verse for urban poetry and satire, yet he unfortunately spawned too many rural-clones during and after his demise. It is often forgotten, or disregarded that Kavanagh hated his local village, well not hated one hundred percent, but if you read his poetry, the hatred outweighs the love of the countryside: he found refuge in the city, if inferiority as he was recognisably rural, unlike H who quit the farmstead for education and a progressively successful career in teaching at many levels where he could promote himself as Faberman.

Across the Irish Sea, poets such as Dylan Thomas and R. M. Thomas, H's older contemporaries hold the field in twentieth-century pastoral English poetry because they did more with the form than H's farmyard-museum verse of churning butter, closing gates, milking cows and admiring the scenery. H is a smaller clone-version of the many Kavanagh clones who still operate in Ireland. Admittedly, archaic nostalgic rural imagery is a staple of Irish verse even today, and H is currently (or just about) the yardstick for academic 'poetry' on campus of this type.

H's verse has no affinities with the two Thomas poets, he hails from the media era that raised Pam Ayres to 'famous' TV poet with accessible punch-line verse, occasional bawdy subject matter with double entendres, and excessive use of her rustic accent for added comic effect. Ayres, in turn, echoed the flower-toting 'poet' Henry Gibson of Rowan and Martyn's *Laugh-In* whose verses included deliberate cringe comedy verse such as "Dogs are better than Ants (as Pets)". H soon lost his accent on the academic circuit to the normal whine of the campus professor but I always place him with Ayres and Gibson. However, I assert that this text is hardcore academic analysis to counter the claims for H as poet.

H became Faber property in a publishing house meeting the crisis of gross lack of talent after their golden era. William Oxley described British poetry in critical terms retrospectively in the 1990s, reducing the deflated repute of Brian Patten, Jeni Couzyn, Andrew Motion and Craig Raine along with 'the recently hyped Wendy Cope and Simon Armitage' (Ox, 10). The poetry business in public reputation making is a sorry state of affairs tied up with careers, salaries, editors, publishers and academic power. Faber's 'own' Raine, Motion and Armitage presume the achievement of classical poets such as Blake, Byron, Wordsworth, Coleridge, Shelley, Hardy, the WWI Poets including David Jones, Keith Douglas and Robert Graves, as well as the Poundian, Basil Bunting among others. As I write, Faber is strategically run by Lacklan Mackinnon and Wendy Cope, aka Mrs and Mrs Faber.

One may as well say, run into the ground: be assured that contemporary British poets of worth, are not being published by Faber. If you check out the verse of Cope & Mackinnon, you will understand my position immediately. Cope is 'famous' for synopsising *The Waste Land* into a couple of Limericks. Mackinnon is 'famous' for 'poems' that look uncannily like diary entries. Faber has become the cruellest mammoth. However, when they put out classic poets, the introductions are done by feeble contemporaries all Faber personnel, thus making the ultimate pretence to continuity. Faber's actions are those of Poetry & Poetry Unlimited which is their arch claim.

Thus H's 'imposed' presence by certain vested interests is what I shall expose. The truth is that as time grinds on, H will be located in the position assigned him here just as Thomas Moore was declared to have squeezed the harp into a snuff box. Moore is, of course, far better (if bygone) than H. The professoriate in the majority pretend to admire H, yet, very few of them will 'out him'; however, the few who have, are listed below. My sympathy is for students and others, who are being forcibly steered towards H's verse, and whose time is being wasted on this tenth rate fraud.

H, is in fact, a very easy target but his detrimental effects require addressing. I (optimistically) know that unwary users of poetry (young and old) may have to dabble with him in educational institutions, and prescribed at second and third levels. The majority of such users pass him by rapidly, once they have handed in their paper on *Beowulf* or 'Northern Ireland Poetry of the Troubles Era' and 'H's archaeological transpositions'. It is a great insult to the dead from the North of Ireland War (1968-1998) that H and so-called *Northern poets* were seen, and are still to some extent as representative of the war when their verse barely dabbles with the immensity of it.

H, without academic acceptance is unthinkable as a verse-property. H *sans* the stale curricula of his era would have been a non-starter since critics have shown that he misrepresents a genre of English nature-verse rather than being distinctly Irish. H, in his verse is inaccurate, mealy-mouthed, rhetorical and laden in sophistry, using language that is clumsy with words, and in love with his own voice. H's fast-food fodder verse was lapped up primarily by many lazy professors, indicative of their lack of critical integrity besmirching the wider vistas of the academy.

The core of criticism is hierarchy, explication, and erudition, as to what is valuable for woman, man, society, country, and the world-making of literature. Literature is a parallel world in our world, not something to be endured by complicit students, and merely utilitarian towards the degree process and job market, tokenism as a forgotten sojourn within itself: literature is more than alive to those who experience it. My case is not a protest because poetry is secure but at the level of injustice, I am lodging the complaint, conscience-bound but wish to get back to work, however, this chore had to be addressed.

I am giving literature its full status and outing one of the major counterfeiters of my generation. However, I am not a solitary voice, as was loudly heard in Trinity College Dublin in 2013, at the Ezra Pound International conference. Loudly heard by me, however, as not many publish what they hold to critically about H. His supporters may outnumber those who out him but this is changing rapidly.

H was invited to speak in TCD in 2013, being a 'brand name' and in truth his address on Pound, was, to be kind—graduate level, and poorly put together. As a member of the organising committee, I voted for H as a plenary speaker, in order not to seem reactive. To my utter satisfaction, I recall the lunch that day, hearing the majority of voices and their opinion of H as writer: 'half-penny Poundian' said one of the professors.

I had a cup of coffee with H and his wife, Marie. My walking tour of literary Dublin had caught their attention, and which I admitted was 'literary fun' leading the academic pack to the city's significant glittering streets and locations, associated with Swift, Wilde, Shaw, O'Casey, Synge, Yeats, Stoker, and Joyce to name only some. H was his usual diplomatic avuncular self, smiling, hand-shaking like a politician, but well I knew how these Poundians actually considered H's verse, and the tattered lecture he'd delivered with a string of quotes that any anthology could provide from Pound. H doesn't have to be rated as a scholar, but then again one would expect a verse-maker of his innings, to at least strike some fire from Pound. Many of us kept polite, nodded, smiled ironically, and felt some sort of obeisance had been made to none other than Faber & Faber really, for H was their so-called stable winner but as will be shown, far from classic material. This I knew many years ago.

H's verse represents the diminution of literature to something that is mere novelty, nostalgia, anecdote, lame joke and faded photograph-album memory. H is a verse maker of dead objects within a dead noisy misuse of language, guttural showy word-effects backed up by the house of Faber, based on their former pedigree as publisher of notable twentieth century poets. H's explanations and dramatic pleas based on his Mossbawn farmyard never recreates the beautiful landscape of the region of North Derry, and indeed close by North Antrim: spectacular places; nor does he infuse the sectarian foreground into his literary output as did Padraic Fiacc and James Simmons. H is a repository of fake literature unleashed and to some extent imprinted but not indelible and all because of his seeing a pump erected in the farmyard. H is the pretence of gold that is straw, milk that is whitewash, water that is dirty. This is, I must repeat, not *ad hominem* but at his product in verse. Product is linguistically overstating it.

I: Heaney in bed with Helen Vendler

One of his champions among the professoriate is Helen Vendler, as a name it sounds like 'vendor' which she became, and she makes my case in giving the game away in her 1998 publication which in turn buries the exegesis of H's verse in imprecise critical language. There are implications beyond language, in the realm of abuse of poetic culture, by calling it poetry. It is like any mis-representation that uses sophistry or rhetoric. This is as much the failure of HU in financing the lifelong Vendler, beginning with her PhD on Yeats under the tutelage of the gifted Professor John V. Kelleher which proves the limitations of the academic quagmire, but she is not alone in being dangerous to poetry, and being dull as ditchwater in its assessment, if you examine her tome on Emily Dickinson. H loathed Dickinson's poetry; on being asked about a line of his, obviously derived from one of her poems, he coyly remarked: 'I don't know whether to be happy or unhappy about it' (StepStone 289). A poet would not deny Dickinson anything.

Not surprisingly, Faber siphoned off Dickinson, and handle her *Collected Poems* for the European English speaking world, and Hughes did a *Selected Poems* of Dickinson. Business is business of course but my case is the *emperor's new clothes* schools of verse masquerading as poetry.

In dealing with H, one is in the same ditchwater (mentioned above). Unfortunately, a few notable professors cannot redeem the academies. Professors in the majority, rule over academy curricula, hence the following: 'And there are poems of selfhood (notably "The Badgers") that I will reserve for consideration of Heaney's alter egos in the next chapter (Vendler 74).' Of course, one understands this but its pseudo-scientific diatribe is pernicious and really doesn't matter in its content, based upon commenting about H's effusions; 'effusions' is too complimentary a term for his verse. I have returned to complete this book-length essay having been woken up fully a long time ago to H, as one of the feeblest verse-makers of the twentieth century. Almost any page of Vendler yields similar useless fodder: 'he has levelled his voice to the conversational, turned his anthropological gaze to the ordinary ways life is lived, and become able, as a fieldworker, to sketch psychological and cultural transactions' (Vendler 74). There is a diminution of country life in Vendler that is abhorrent since many universities are in pastoral locations and with employees who would be more capable of commenting on the paucity of response by H to rural values, horticulture and nature.

Look at it 'levelled'; 'anthropological gaze' and 'fieldworker'. I require some sort of relief after the nausea of Vendler. Her analysis of "The Badgers" refers to 'the numinous presence poem'[...] 'addressing himself, imagines the invisible but sensed badger as a revenant compounded of the murdered and the murderer' (Vendler 90). This is so loathsome, sad, and dispiritingly awful, and fraudulent as language usage that it is disgusting. I will prove that H hijacked the Sectarian War (1968-1998) in Ireland, and dined out on it; lived off it, kept away from its fiery centre, and yet made the prosperous claim to being its voice and assumed this role. Furthermore, snippets of H became the ideal filler by tabloid journalists during the war. These filler quotes made an easy accessible rural nostalgia to soften what were undeniably the sufferings, agony, strife, and deaths unfolding month by month, year by year, and in commentary on the war from the news media. Anyone who believed (and many did at the time) that H could represent the war's texture, intensity, and complexity obviously knew nothing about the North of Ireland during this period. Invariably, H as verse-maker evoking nature, farmyards and animals, with a smattering of diluted reality suited those who wished to avoid the fierce wartime events.

H's backslapping, self-serving critics are such a breed, who granted him this role. Their disservice to poetry is tinged in deprivation, and the malevolence of keeping students bound to such a turgid non-poet, for that is my thesis, and having been minced through the academic process myself, suffered the fakery on my psyche of such a fog of verse which is survivable, even to the point of laughter, disgust and derision, except for the touch of evil in terms of embezzlement of finding one's time wasted on useless professoriate-babble that counterfeits criticism and promotes non-poetry.

I will return to Vendler, and do not have to waste much of the reader's time, re-hashing the complete commentary of hyperbole from other critics who pedalled H as academic fodder, except for a brief distillation of his superannuated fans who perpetuate the hoax, including John Carey, Frank Kermode, Peter Levi, Karl Miller, Blake Morrison, Andrew Motion, Lachlan Mackinnon, Christopher Ricks and Harold Bloom. The fact that these embrace H among real poets whom they 'teach' academic courses on, calls into question their critical discrimination. There is the whole area in any event, of the faculty and its presumed critical faculty, especially if it lumps H in with genuinely canonical poets. I loathe terms like canon and core: they involve the curricula. Placing H on any curriculum means real literature is being defrauded.

Clive James and Stephen Fry are in another media-poetry zone. James was an early 'admirer' of H, being himself a closet writer of verse as TV personality who presumed Faber & Faber could develop his verse product, but as it happened, he moved in on Picador and began to steer their ship. Clive James translated Dante which Picador peddles—the translation is a hellish experience on earth from what one garners—glancing at random through it. Fry is the terribly sincere, liberal goody-goody, among the plethora of 'renaissance men' TV personalities, an actor, writer, host, comedian 'heck' cetera, and in *The Ode Less Travelled* (note the Spike Milligan title) expounds on poetry, and of course, praises H.

This is sinking pretty low, having to quote Fry, but I will refrain from quoting Clive James: both are similar verbose lightweights. H's: 'superb poem "The Outlaw", which might be regarded as a kind of darkly ironic play on an *eclogue* or *georgic*—Virgilian verse celebrating and philosophically discoursing upon the virtues of agricultural life' (Fry, 207). This reflects Fry's diffuse language and amounts to no-meaning, except he shows that he links H to Virgil's *Eclogues*. H must be Homeric for his promoters in order to fool the public: he must be their Seamus Homer and Virgil Heaney. Note the imprecision in 'a kind of darkly ironic play' which is not untypical of 'media arts' panel discussions, inclusive of Melvyn Bragg and others, who attempt to hold sway with media-opinionated views on 'poetry'.

Here is Fry, once more and finally, and who continually moralises between his expositions on poets who 'drank themselves to death', or are 'deeply unstable and unhappy neurotic', as if other humans do not share such chaos, but of course H is above this, and can provide a villanelle along with 'some very funny examples by Wendy Cope demonstrate that it need not be always down in the dumps' (Fry, 228).

Back to business. Examine the H Bibliography (2008) and note the number of his supporters who continually reviewed him; and he them. Richard Ellmann, Brian Friel, and Ted Hughes were extensively reviewed by H. And Robert Lowell eight times. H puffed his fellow Northern verse men. John Montague twelve times back-slaps H; Paul Muldoon six times; and Peter Fallon, H's Irish publisher. H is praising of Fallon in a tribute in the *Irish Literary Supplement* (1995). The verse men club coterie is another aspect, fully ascertainable from the H Bibliography, a doorstop book from Faber which provides more evidence but I must move on.

I am not a pioneer in declaring H more than 'unfit'. Others precede me with this news, including A. N. Wilson, A. A. Alvarez, Carol Rumens, James Simmons and Andrew Waterman. Simmons was the keenest contemporary critic in writing "The Trouble with Seamus". Realising and outing the H hoax, Simmons took issue with 'the madness of reviewers such as John Carey'; Waterman rejects any comparison between H and Lowell; David Lloyd ranks H as 'a minor poet [...] elevated to a touchstone of contemporary taste' (Sammells, 282). Simmons accurately gauged the hoax, stating that H 'was preparing books for Faber'; John Lucas and Desmond Fennell place H politically as silent, and inexplicably during a thirty-year war on his far off doorstep, however H fled to the Southern comfort of the Irish Republic (Sammells, 283).

Simmons exposes the fact that "At Ardboe Point" is typical of H's non-erotic skill in verse: 'Heaney almost talked about sex' (Sammells, 283). Thomas Kinsella was unconvinced by the hoax, seeing the H-factor as part of the 'Northern Ireland [...] renaissance [...] largely a journalistic entity' (Kinsella, xxviii). Jahan Ramazani noted that the perception of H as voice for the victims of sectarian war through verse about another country and time, is 'an artificial parallel between them and ancient sacrificial Danish bog victims' (Brearton and Gillis, 561).

I am opposed to the censorship of literature, and therefore do not symbolically burn H's books on a soggy turf fire, but implicitly I am bound to the protection of real literature in criticism. Criticism is non-institutional, and shuns rhetoric paid for by a consensus-clique promoting favourable criticism with cheques. I am not involved in any institution in writing this work of criticism, therefore I enjoy the full freedom of expression. The criticism of poetry must achieve an ethics of quality control. I am equally opposed to ersatz and counterfeit-literature, in this case H's verse product. Unfortunately, all of the pro-H block of critics are circumstantially bought; their asses, to use the pejorative word, are owned by various establishments and publishers. It is an admiration society, just as Faber has become a protectorate-insider, trader on its past since Faber was, but is not currently, 'one of the world's greatest publishing houses' in terms of literature. Subtract the greats from Faber's past, and you are left with little in terms of the production of poetry. But, if you actually subscribe and admire H's media friendly verse, it is not a case of why not, rather, why would you when there is the cornucopia of real poetry available. Hierarchies aside, the H-factor has largely polluted a certain strand of 'poetry' and my concerns include curricula, students, and the hostage readers in schools and institutions who are compulsorily forced to read this brand of fake verse, and why textbook makers promote H as a viable, appraisable 'poet'.

Neil Corcoran's book is from Faber (Weird & Weird), and is a standard academic text on H: abominable stuff which is a punishment to inflict on any reader. The appendix makes my case about H's controlled politics from the start of his verse career. H published "Intimidation" in *The Malahat Review* (no. 17, 1970); note the year 1970, for the verse was thereafter suppressed by H himself, and did not appear in *Wintering Out* or *North* since by then he was a bought Faberman, and would not have been permitted to publish such as the following stanza concerning loyalist thugs who march and make bonfires as intimidation to nationalists in the North of Ireland; significantly the title is "Intimidation":

Ghetto rats! Are they the ones

To do the smoking out?

They'll come streaming past

To taste their ashes yet (Corcoran 251)

For once, in these lines H was politically supportive of his tribe, if rhetorically, but H never fully supported his tribe in his verse ever afterwards, and made a complete *volte face* away from anything that seemed anti-British with respect to the thirty year war in the North of Ireland. It cannot be stressed enough that signing on the dotted line for Faber meant becoming English for H, indeed a situation not untrue of a minority of Irish nationalists 'stuck' in the North of Ireland; H was able to escape but not in his verse-career.

Even the war was reduced by the media, and always referred to it as 'the Troubles', a kind of parlance for a spot of bother. The moral laxity of H, is not that any writer should have made an imperative of addressing the war, but his assumed and presumed stance was associated with the war. In the media he was the war poet of the North of Ireland but in actuality he was of no-stance ultimately in politics. H happily assumed a false position, cheered on by academics who as shameful cowards on culture-salaries, did not want to discuss bombs, bullets, and what was part of history unfolding in the six counties of Ireland, once the underclass of Catholic nationalists sought equal rights, civil rights and human rights, and their public peaceful demonstrations by bodies such as NICRA who found willing members to join the Republican armed struggle against militant loyalists, the British Army, the SAS, MI5 and the RUC during the war.

H, not once reflects the setting up of the six counties by Britain's arming the Ulster Volunteers in 1912, and thereafter Britain's supporting the covertly militarised loyalist communities of the Six Counties who were not subjected to the same laws as nationalists with regard to owning weapons. Basic North of Ireland history reveals such details, but H is camouflaged in nature writing, in the midst of his publishing history. All through the 30 years war, he published meagre verse based on a folksy rural Ireland, already bygone—the invention of minor writers such as H—and not even the rural life of the actual wartime era of 1968-1998. H's glance was backwards, and beyond to ancient archaeology, and far away from his homeland which he falsifies.

I met H on a number of occasions as a human being, in that one can evaluate people at random; he was a 'good man' but in the realm of verse as 'bad' as his admirers, forming a shallow collective if not protectorate, based on the end of an era at Faber & Faber. A sinking ship with sinking talents. Obviously, one does not have to rehearse here the golden and silver ages of F&F, from Eliot to Beckett, from Berryman to Sylvia Plath. H himself, on having his first collection Faberised, says it all, in realising the scam: 'The actual book looked very good: a lime green and solid-pink-dust jacket, and on the back a list of Faber poets. Fabulous names' (StepStone 61). He'd slipped in via Charlie Monteith, T. S. Eliot's understudy from the halcyon days when poets were poets in Faber. Monteith was, of course the beginning of the end for Faber in terms of poetry; Monteith as cosy fireside verse-lover assessing poetry, in that he went for H's product and pushed such verse into the network. In so doing, he 'bought' H whose politics was in any event shallow and ultimately became pro-Unionist. There is a moral dilemma for Ireland and Irish nationalists that live in the six sectarian counties of Ulster where Loyalist triumphalism is supported economically and bought. This fact of life is continually airbrushed out of centre stage media discussion as it was immediately not even brought into question by H and Monteith. H had to be steered from the start into a pro-British position by becoming a Southern Irish conservative and what used to be termed in the first-half of the twentieth century by Irish Republicans as West-British.

I will quote Vendler and a lesser light, Dillon Johnston whose luminosity is not considered to shine as brightly as Harvard professors. I lump in Ted Hughes with H, making it H&H from F&F

(Faber & Faber) who followed the gifted poets of Lowell, Berryman, Plath and very few others after the golden age of Eliot, Pound, Muir and Auden. F&F's obvious commercial venture in pushing H&H really began once Plath had become a phenomenon. In reality, Hughes is her inferior in poetry to his better contemporaries: Donald Davie, Francis Berry, Anthony Twaite, Bernard Spencer, Charles Tomlinson, John Gurney, Francis Warner, Alexis Lykiard, David Grubb, Geoffrey Godbert or even Fred Beake.

When Fleur Adcock got up F&F's *Twentieth Century Women's Poetry* proving that gender wars aided their verse market, it is the Americans who shine through, for the muse almost fully deserted Britain and Ireland for America distinctly after WWII but there is British (to use Adcock's term) women's poetry of H's era but I am straying from my main theme. This point is substantiated if not admitted by Adcock in that of her 64 poets in the Faber anthology, 25 are British.

Vendler, is by no means alone in her crimes against language, her infringements of youthful students right to real literature, in that how many have been turned off poetry by such diatribes as the following, in murdering and dissecting the rubbish-lines from H in his self-promoting "Elegy" to Robert Lowell:

helmsman, netsman, *retiarius*.

That hand. Warding and grooming

and amphibious... [FW 32]

Vendler is of course on hand, to explain all 'this' in pseudo-lingo:

"Helmsman" because of Lowell's transatlantic passage after his third marriage ('You were our night ferry'); "netsman" because of his words in *The Dolphin* about writing ('I've gladdened a lifetime/knotting, undoing a net of tarred fishrope'); '*retiarius*' (a gladiator who worked with a net) because Lowell's encounter with 'the ungovernable and dangerous', and because of his inveterate returns to Latinity in language; the 'hand' because it was always in motion forward and back as Lowell talked, a barrier and an emphasis, 'amphibious' because it moved both in the dry land of prose and in the surges of metaphor [...] (Vender 62)

What BS this is. So H's verse is a crossword puzzle, and Vendler holds the answers to the clues that are already built into H's verse; and indeed H's profession as teacher ensured that his effusions are wordy-crossword verse, adopting a sort of TV *Batman* screen sensationalism, using words as visual captions. There is nothing in Vendler but academic-speak about academic verse. This is such self-defeating twaddle for every gentle student who is forced to 'study' such language and is violence against, and denial of real poetry to the student. Veldler and H are working against the beauty of language, its logic, communication, visionary efflux, and reason for being language. Vendler is a purveyor of the pompous print era, peddling the depravity of bad-language in fake professorial expertise.

To state it clearly, Vendler and her tribe are deliberate in their criticism that is putrefying the dialect just as H's verse does. Mallarmé's dictate was about 'giving a purer sense to the words of the tribe' (Mallarmé 18) but I am not giving in to manifestos. Vendler is 'valuable' as an example to 'out' the lazy infertile miasma, I mean just that: the profusion of unfruitful commentators 'writing' during tenured-salaried vacations as cultural tourists, however, to gather together H and her in the following, further exposes their collective vileness. This is where she and H justify the farmyard pump (of all things) in that she posits as his 'centre, the *omphalos*, of the child's world' (Vendler 174). H's pump in childhood is the primal pump of all pumps: the mother and father of all pumps, indeed pump-ness as a pseudo-physical and metaphysical entity. This is a disgusting perversion of language and content in pseudo-analytical hyperbole.

H in *Preoccupations* (1980) while elaborating (God help us), gives it all away as he frames this redundant image of the farm, farmyard, and cottage infrastructure that are his stock in trade (literally), and namely his hallowed pump:

> There the pump stands, a slender, iron idol, snouted, helmeted...I remember...men coming to sink the shaft of the pump...That pump marked an original descent into earth, sand, gravel, water. It centred and staked the imagination, made its foundation, the foundation of the *omphalos* itself (qtd. in Vendler 174).

This is such a preposterous load of codswallop, ultimately borrowed from the epic opening to Joyce's *Ulysses* where 'omphalos' is granted a multilayered symbolism when Dedalus imagines the poet and critic, Matthew Arnold, and in fact, prefigures Ireland's coming into 'ourselves...newpaganism...omphalos' (*Ulysses* 7). H's usage is presumably not from reading the novel but from academic commentaries, so he plumps for making an *omphalos* out of this most unlikely water-conduit in a farmyard (how cutesy! how clichéd!) and as usual in a linguistic menagerie of confusion.

It presents the sort of slow thinking academic vagueness suggestive of unclear images, windy phrases, and the use of hollow language. H was, of course, involved from the start of his Faberization in keeping a parallel commentary on his own work through published remarks, interviews, and asides to admiring academics and journalists, in a

The Beats and Black Mountain Poets: 'I just couldn't leave the gravitational pull of the poetry field I knew, couldn't slip the halter of the verse line and the stanza' (StepStone 145). He has to use words like 'field' and 'halter': farmyard trademark terms. A single pump action versifier true to his 'invented' idiolect.

Appointed to the Southern Irish Arts Council in 1973 (StepStone 153) H first met Conor Cruise O'Brien in 1967 'when I was teaching in Trinity College Summer School' (StSt 154). This establishes his conservative politics, associating with a coward like Cruise O'Brien the pro-Burkean who hated, dreaded and proselytised against the French Revolution. O'Brien loathed Thomas Jefferson and saw him thus: 'the card of the French Revolution was a winning card in American politics and Jefferson played it with aplomb' (COB 387). O'Brien failed to understand the Irish republican traditions, propagandised against them rendering his viewpoints as nil when in fact he joined and became active in the UK Unionist Party. 'Tony O'Reilly, whose views concerning the influence of Sinn Féin-IRA were closely similar to my own' (COB 380). O'Brien noted the Maze prisoners hunger strike as follows 'ten members of the IRA, serving prison terms for violent offences, starved themselves to death' (COB 415).

O'Brien who had once been a Minister in the Irish Government Dáil Eireann, latterly in 1995 became a canvasser for Robert McCartney of the Unionists, this of course emphasised O'Brien's hypocrisy since as he admitted 'the UUP cultivates close relations with the political fronts of two loyalist paramilitary groups' (COB 431) afraid to name them of course—UVF, UDA—but he does chorus his other loyalist friend: 'I found Dr Paisley personally most friendly, and even genial, on our first meeting' (COB 432). Paisley was a supreme promoter of Loyalist sectarian murders through his public speeches inciting hatred during the war against 'Papists' 'Taigs' 'Fenians'. O'Brien's memoir repeatedly calls for opposition to 'reform of the

RUC' and rails about safeguarding policies of British administrations 'with the immediate objective of protecting the RUC' (COB, 444; 445). O'Brien concluded his pro-Unionist memoir in 1998; the RUC were disbanded and replaced by a police force known as the PSNI which has staunch RUC roots.

H bought a copy of the *The Bog People* in 1969, and fell for the pop-archaeology that informs his verse in *North* (StepStone 157). His descriptions are based on the photography in such books, making him a cultural tourist. H ludicrously quotes Pound's instruction trying to gain some Poundian girth: 'Pay no attention to the criticism of those who have not themselves "produced notable work"' (StepStone 162) and cites Kavanagh's *The Great Hunger* and Hughes "The Bull Moses" as prime influences: 'It's what I was mostly after in the beginning in my own writing' (StepStone 193). But on Yeats, he admits tellingly 'great work like that cannot be emulated' (StepStone 195). Obviously, H and Yeats, never the twain shall meet in terms of achievement, but of course, Vendler peddles their parity as recently 'the greatest Irish poet since Yeats, was in 1995 awarded the Nobel Prize "for works of lyrical beauty and ethical depth, which exalt everyday miracles and the living past"' (Foley 9). Sounds as if it was written by H himself but who fears these committee-statements cobbled together with the absurd phrase 'ethical depth' which is vague and indicative of the vast sophistry surrounding H whose era was drowned in imprecise use of language.

Glanmore in his work references the Ann Saddlemyer house, basically a wealthy American with property in Ireland loaning her premises to H, and which he eventually bought outright. H's real muse was the sort of property coveted by the arts establishment and this meant a career to finance it. Carleton is sighted from his birthplace in Tyrone which also reveals H for what he is: a flagrant nostalgia addict: 'It was like driving into your own yard at home, a whitewashed house, a door opening directly on to the street, a life whitewash of real events. Unfortunately, Carson lacks any satirical or critical stance and one may as well leave aside all aesthetics, since reviewing H favourably is anathema to actual poetry or substantial verse. However, Carson too went the way of all fledglings and took a job as lecturer in the Seamus Heaney Centre at Queens University Belfast. The real truth about H's *North* was that for many it supplanted the real North and the war, but those who championed H were happier with weak verse rather than reality. It was an Orwellian time in Ireland, both North and South with commentators like H and Cruise O'Brien listened to for their avoidance, repression and ultimate consolidation of the British imperial stance on the Six Counties as the correct viewpoint and policy. H provided valuable pro-British Newspeak being 'Irish'.

H's *The Government of the Tongue* has huge difficulties as text, lacking cohesion and is replete with phrases meant to be profound but lack meaning, as in his summation of Zbigniew Herbert 'with all the strengths of an Antaeus, yet he finally emerges more like the figure of an Atlas' (GOT 70). Alright one may lapse but in building a discourse, it is not permissible to have unwieldy paragraphs throughout. There is a constant use of diffuseness that has no meaning: it is so cluttered with compounds, as on Eliot's moving on to write *Four Quartets* 'this was a poet very different from the one who wrote *The Waste Land*, one who turned from an earlier trust in process and image to embrace the claims of argument and idea' (GOT 98). This sort of writing is detrimental to any student forced to read such commentary, and there is actually a horrible super-ego, and the sound of an echoing voice back to H himself, that is unethical, in that a writer of verse should not debauch language as being a thing of noise and of no meaning. H does cite a killer phrase from Eliot in a famous letter to E. Martin Browne about 'this solitary toil which often seems so pointless' (qtd in GOT 107) but the poet of *The Waste Land* found a world readership focused on the poet's modernist terrors and breakdowns that corresponded to the readers' terrors and breakdowns, whereas H is a writer of enthusiastic melodramatic hyperbolic verse about nostalgia for a vague mis-articulated childhood. There is no anguish, no struggle, no passion, no extremes of any sort, especially, no extremities of language, insight, thought or emotion.

H's non-emotion in each verse is singularly 'felt' even in his commentary where there is a revealing relegation of his, when discussing Sylvia Plath's "Daddy". H and his own father could not yield anything of value in verse, so H is naturally shocked at the lack of repression in Plath. Poets are not repressed. Yes, they can shock. The shock of H is different because it relates to so many pages of slight useless verse, and as to how such can have gathered its international response: careerism is one answer, however the flaccidity of the audience can be explained by academic consensus. H was easy fodder and living 'poet'; an easy choice for student and academic teacher. But, as for the real poet, as in Plath, yes, this poetry can shock, not that 'shock' is the primary *vade mecum* of a poet and poetry. Yes, the tone of voice and nuance and even conversation can sound shocking to people who are not poets, not artists. Poets are in the minority and labelled as difficult, trouble-makers and loud mouths, where H was handshakes, and smiles that looked as if they'd crack his face in dimples.

H's attack on Plath is proof of his not having a sensibility, and, one has to believe that the intensity of her poem, and its emotional disturbance were states of mind and being unknown to him. I don't mean to single out Plath's poem: what a pity H didn't choose some other poem but H set to explicating "Daddy" and the comments reveal him, not her. The poem according to H 'is so entangled in biographical circumstances and rampages so permissively in the history of other people's sorrows that it simply overdraws its rights to our sympathy' (GOT, 165). For 'other's people's sorrows' of course you can immediately read his buddy Hughes who raged at the

Plath reputation that engulfed Hughes. Factually, historically and realistically, Hughes was a bully and having learnt of Plath's sensitively psychotic nature and fragility, easily swotted her like an insect. However, Plath remains it must be admitted, not by the reputation of dumped wife but immortal poet. H's partisan comment slyly playing buddy to Hughes, his fellow Faber buddy has a touch of evil, for it denies human experience and wishes to confine it, in fact to censor it. H, reflexively in flinging this weak comment at "Daddy" denies the extremities of life, denies the emotional resonances of life which a poet miraculously can render and echo in poetry. Plath's terrors and psychosis can be laughed at behind the hand by those who wish to mock but this fragility finds readers and when compared with H's forced drivel in verse: you cannot find a sensitive syllable in his pages.

The Plath finalé in poetry produced work such as "Lady Lazarus", "Edge", "Little Fugue" and "Daddy" admittedly a portent-poetry extended from her lifelong subconscious wish as she closed her doors, even on her infant children, and walked to her death not unlike to an execution. The poems are what Whitman would have called as he did of Poe's 'melodious expressions, and perhaps never-excell'd ones, for certain pronounc'd phrases of human morbidity' (Whitman 306). Thus Plath's: 'A man in black with a Meinkamph look' (*Ariel* 56). I dare say, Whitman's sensibility would mean that he could have easily taken his hat off to her, and would have sensed that behind the naked confessionalism was the articulation of her crisis, pain and convulsions sustained within art towards suicide. Plath has the power to shock because poetry has the power to shock among other potential and through the sublime shock of beauty.

What I receive from Plath is the beauty of language in an emotional storm and hurricane, a torrent of poetry. Yes, poetry can be this tempestuous in the hands of an artist. If you deny Plath her torpor and its expression, you are inhuman and you become the actual bully that she calls out in her poem. "Daddy" is such an emotional complexity as to be classical and paradoxically clear yet ultimately beyond final explanation. It is this infinity that a poem presents. I don't need to quote Plath's poem (in full) or extrapolate on the other poems mentioned above, and that they actually form a frieze within her work. This is my point, H in being a vile counterfeiter of so-called 'poetry' aided by his admirers is easily revealed as charlatan when discussing real poetry.

H in denying Plath's poetry and by denying one of her masterpiece-works in saying such, is a flawed critic. Hopeless indeed. This is someone abusing the act of criticism, and cheapening the act of criticism as if the criticism of poetry is mere showy language, a showy speech at a prize giving when everyone is expected to listen to you, for such is the auspicious day. H, fundamentally can be outed because a real poet is equally a real critic of poetry: this is provable from the history of poetry. Thus, H's abuse of Plath is revolting, it makes his so-called *government of the tongue*, one that is here exposed as foul-mouthed against poetry itself, foul mouthed against the beauty of poetry, the emotional truths of poetry and the excellent diction of poetry as language reaching perfection.

Plath's poem is so true to her life that it never 'overdraws its rights to our sympathy'. Never to all eternity: how many women and men has one not heard rail against a father, as Plath does, hence the universality of the poem. Behind Plath's poem is a greater truth about the toxic parent, the parent who ultimately destroys their child as family legacy. H could not in his sentimental versifying ever have reached such insights and indeed never did. H's verses about his Da, are mere Christmas Card verse beside Plath's. I also contest that her poetry is beyond sibling-parental psychic upheaval as a vital presence in lives under threat from self-destruction. Her poems cannot one hundred per cent save lives (if advertisers believed that Faber & Faber would really parade further fakery), but I can believe

walking or cycling) about the landscape, wasting petrol in his search for cute metaphors. To uncode a landscape actually has no meaning. H is using it to pretend that he, as versifier has a special Da Vinci code for de-coding landscape. The real problem is that if this was a nature poem about a peninsula it would bring you there, and make you feel it, anything but H's silent mumbling of noisy words.

"Requiem for the Croppies" is indicative of his miniscule, loose approach in sonnet forms. So little is referred to about the 1798 Rebellion in Wexford as to be futile, but he can't resist the urge to pretence about history: 'The priest lay behind ditches with the tramp' (NSP 66-87; 12) which is meant to mark the famous priest from Ballymurphy of the Rebellion but the verse misfires with trite remarks like 'The hillside blushed' (NSP 66-87; 12). This is of course meant to be poetic wisdom in reflecting blood as metaphor, and the landscape personified and blushing. It is just a weird, awkward rubbishing of history. H is not interested in Irish history, just as he passes over all Irish poetry, if you note his slight comments on one classic poem by Mangan and only one.

"The Wife's Tale" is also history used as bogus material with his clichéd rural idolatry as in 'The hum and gulp of the thresher ran down' (NSP 66-87; 13). A thresher doesn't actually eat anything and making it human is ridiculous. "Night Drive" is an example of his hyper-bland hyperbole as a night drive past road signs, where 'Each place granting its name's fulfilment' (NSP 66-87; 15). It is a drive to Italy and the 'biggest' assertion is the schoolboy remark,

'where Italy

Laid its loin to France'. (NSP 66-87; 15).

That's it. The conclusion is 'Your ordinariness was renewed there'. This conclusion wouldn't work on a holiday poster. Drive to the Loin of Italy: 'Your ordinariness will be renewed there'. What he is trying to do, is evoke this passing from one country to another by night, but his words are so dead in the attempt.

"Bogland" makes my point about H-metaphors, the 'H' stands for hysterical, hyperbole and hollow—the elk is compared to 'An astounding crate full of air' (NSP 66-87; 17) and the biggest *faux-pas* is comparing the bogland to 'black butter'. Come on, this is an abuse of language: bogland is not butter of any colour. The real conspiracy involves those critics who collectively presumed the following: 'Anticipating the supporting evidence of P. V. Glob's *Bog People*, which Heaney read in 1969, he had represented the bog as a repository where the past is rendered contemporaneous with the present' (PAJ 141-2). This is the apotheosis of counterfeit, making verse and badly out of the archaeology of bog corpses, in fact based on photographs seen in a book and in a museum.

Yes, poetry could be kick-started from anything but H's verse was pushed into being read by his cowardly admirers, as a gloss on the North of Ireland War. There were many repetitions of this fraudulence in "Bog Oak" that has the disagreeableness of the one about the croppies. In "Bog Oak" the English poet Spenser is injected into the lines as cheaply as a pair of old socks from Marks & Spencer. H then squeezes in nine words from Spenser's book including the archaic spelling 'woodes and glennes' (NSP 66-87; 20) about Ireland amidst the 'mizzling rain' (NSP 66-87; 19); 'mizzling' is a coinage of drizzle and mist: how ingenious. The invocation to Spenser, if it can be called that, is absurd, 'Perhaps I just make out/Edmund Spenser' (NSP 66-87; 19). No you don't, you plastic ersatz bog-man.

The linguistically self-conscious H is nauseating as in the local hill "Anahorish" that gives its name to another 'poem' where it is 'vowel-meadow' (NSP 66-87; 21). "Gifts of Rain" is self-regarding about how he learns from rainfall because of his need 'for antediluvian lore' (NSP 66-87; 23). Dreadfully self-conscious. "Broagh" is another linguistic-bout of self-consciousness, except this time he asserts locality and pushes being a local yokel because

gh the strangers found

difficult to manage. (NSP 66-87; 25).

H means: strangers find it difficult to pronounce the last syllable of Broagh. Astonishing his ear for the stranger, isn't it? "A New Song" is about local place where 'stepping stones like black molars' (NSP 66-87; 27). Note the metaphor, woefully inaccurate. H is no surrealist, or, is so by misappropriation. But one 'knows' his implication for the following which is non-rational and false:

our river tongues must rise

From licking deep in native haunts (NSP 66-87; 27).

"The Other Side" uses his stock-in-trade anecdotal format when a shy neighbour ventures to drop in when the Catholic rosary is being said. His speech is given:

I was dandering by

and says I, I might as well call. (NSP 66-87; 29).

It moves to a sentimental ending as do all his anecdotal pieces. This Irish rural life folklore is done 'better' by Brian MacMahon, Alice Taylor and John B. Keane if you really need such reading material. "The Tollund Man" much praised by his admirers, is actually a form of invented anecdote about Dutch archaeology, bog corpses and cadavers. The apparatus fails him especially the arch lines that admirers have twisted to imply references to the sectarian murders in the North of Ireland war:

Out there in Jutland

In the old man-killing parishes

I will feel lost,

Unhappy and at home (NSP 66-87; 32).

The implied meaning is that for Jutland read the unfortunate Six Counties of NI while H is actually residing in safe, cosy middleclass South of Ireland; all you have to do is check it out in Vendler's timeline. The trick here, for trick it was: H feeling at home, having seen a bog corpse in a foreign museum and brochure. This is completely false as regards factuality and real poetry is not some meaningless mumbo jumbo. There are no Catholic parishes in Jutland. Otherwise, it makes the affinity more with King William of Orange among whose armies were Dutch mercenaries when he used Ireland, typical of English kings to advance their accessions and wars. Is H lamenting by suggestive inference from his admirers about Loyalist deaths? Johnston finds in "The Tollund Man" the primal inspiration for H drawing on Glob's account of a recovered Iron-Age man, sacrificed to an earth goddess and mummified in a Danish bog, he compares this sacrificial death to murder in Ulster (IPAJ, 143).

This is bogus. Illogical. The verse is about what, perhaps a bog corpse and as metaphor by H's cunning interpreters, is transposed from one country to another, and out of joint and time. It might have fooled the supporting critics but not readers of poetry in pleading that H was critically unaware of the hoax involved. Similarly, textbooks follow the received ideas that "The Grauballe Man" like "The Tollund Man" symbolizes 'religious and political violence in Northern Ireland' (*PopCan* 280).

"Wedding Day" is a confused memory where the cake is described as 'tall'. No one speaks of a wedding cake as 'tall'. That's a tall tale, but never that's a 'tall cake' unless you are joking or coming to English as a foreign language. "Summer Home" is about a marital row, a tame one but you can't expect passion or eroticism from H. H has one single effort at an erotic image which I will come to but such material is rare. You could never confuse H for the Marquis de Sade, D. H. Lawrence or Henry Miller. There is no sex in H's stuff at all, unless you count the frogspawn. The claim in "Summer Home" is 'water lives down the tilting stoups of your breasts' (NSP 66-87; 35). You can expect a mammary, farmyard adjective from H in using stoups but the 'tilting' is so obvious and the 'lives' so discordant. 'Water lives' makes weak science. Anyway, the marital row forces H to look backwards to a time when 'Our love calls tiny as a tuning fork.' (NSP 66-87; 36) Get it, kinda like music you know. If music be the food of love, Shakespeare said. You will find nothing Shakespearean in H either.

"Bye-Child" has two H-specials in the metaphor department. The lamp is compared to 'A yolk of light' (NSP 66-87; 38) get it, like an egg, and light is a sort of yellow colour. Extraordinary observation, eh? Wow, did you ever notice that? A photograph is 'Glimpsed like a rodent/On the floor of my mind' (NSP 66-87; 38). This beggars logic really, and as I said, H cannot be viewed as a surrealist: such a denomination is beyond his folkloric parameters.

"Westering" is 'set' in California which fails to snapshot the scenery even the 'Cars stilled outside still churches' (NSP 66-87; 40) is not evocative, and remains clumsy. You cannot expect politics from H, especially since it is understood that 'working' for Faber & Faber meant complete compromise to his statements on the North of Ireland. If you don't have a timeline for the 1968-1998 war, you cannot grasp H's filial position with regards to the London version of newspeak on the reality of 'Gnaw-then Eyeland' as damn'd trouble spot.

"England's Difficulty" hints at the German bombing of Belfast during World War II and is extremely vague. "Trial Runs" is faked about the US troops in the North of Ireland during WWII. H's self-inflicted papist jokes are unfunny, as when an Orange neighbour is giving a pair of rosary beads to H's father, the beads apparently stolen 'off/the pope's dresser when his back was turned' (NSP 66-87; 45). Boarding school and Gaeltacht anecdotes are similarly weak in "Cloistered" and "The Stations of the Cross". The much laboured, much mulled over line is always irritatingly present in H, as in "Mossbawn: Two Poems in Dedication " No. 2. "The Seed Cutters": 'Behind a windbreak wind is breaking through' (NSP 66-87; 51) it seems tautological, so get it, wind is breaking through.

"Funeral Rites" is contemporary because of the juxtaposition of megalithic and Viking burials. Well, ask his admiring critics. Give H a photo of a prehistoric bog corpse and he could update it to Tabloid status before you could say 'Shankill Butchers'. The tired hyperbole includes 'I knelt courteously/admiring it all' (NSP 66-87; 52) because H is, get it within 'the great chambers of Boyne' (NSP 66-87; 53). What reverence from the Nordy tourist, basking in the

Middleclass South. The profundity about death being a constant is pervasively tedious, as is his imagining of the ancient burial rites taking place, which H in any event, could never have witnessed, nor has he any imaginative powers to evoke them. This proxy fake liaison with the megalithic-mythic past is fodder for H's bad verse.

"North" has a similar focus with 'the Atlantic thundering' which is amateur as he faced 'the unmagical/invitations of Iceland' (NSP 66-87; 56) and calls the ancient invaders 'those fabulous raiders' (NSP 66-87; 56). This is his 'inspiration' that tells him to

Lie down

in the word-hoard [...]

Compose in darkness [...]

Keep your eye clear

as the bleb of an icicle (NSP 66-87; 57)

All this is pretentious, fictitious, and with no verbal accuracy. H is always explaining how he is stirred, if not provoked to write these dreadful little squibs of verses. Real truth is that Charlie Monteith was on the phone asking for more bog-lore in chopped up lines. Besides, you cannot lie down in a word-hoard, it is not a form of bedding. Who can respond to this, as any sort of 'poetry' except his gang? It is hardly verse too, except for the 'slightly better' stuff that rarely avoids wordy egotistical vague statements about H's creativity. Keep your eye clear as the bleb of an icicle, is meaningless in reality. This is verse seeking after-effects, and achieving nothing in actuality.

In "Viking Dublin: Trial Pieces" the imprecision begins in Part I, where you cannot be sure what kind of bone from a Viking is seen through a magnified display case at an excavation exhibition (H is poking about in Museums, expect a verse or two on what he has seen!):

the nostril

is a migrant prow

sniffing the Liffey (NSP 66-87; 59).

He has to go for the metaphor. Another awkward H-metaphor. Unreal humans and animals sniff but ghosts have no bones, and bones don't sniff about. He can't resist 'I am Hamlet the Dane,[...] smeller of rot//in the state' (NSP 66-87; 60) choosing the most basic Hamlet quote which is left hanging there. His naivety in alluding to Hamlet is for the academic audience who will nod—O see where H referenced Hamlet with the skull. Wow, the erudition of H is mindblowing. A fascinating parallel professor Bloom, eh?

When part VI of "Viking Dublin: Trial Pieces" enters modern Dublinese, one is impatient to abandon the piece altogether. "Bone Dreams" utilises the same subject matter. H as 'poet-commodity' with a cornered market by Charlie Monteith, saying: 'O yes old chap there is a spot of bother in *Gnaw-then Eyeland* but we have H, and his cosy pomes about digging, fetching water, and all that. What ho!' Frankly, H had to pop out 'poems' like a prize winning verse-chicken for Faber; hence the default verse in his meanderings. In

"Strange Fruit" is part of this grouping, as he appropriates an oblique reference to the song sung by Billie Holiday about racial murders of African-Americans in the US. H luxuriates in showy assonance using a museum description: 'her leathery beauty'. The unfortunate corpse was 'Murdered, forgotten, nameless, terrible/Beheaded girl' (NSP 66-87; 73). Nothing is revealed through the descriptive morass, certainly nothing contemporaneously political, except for his politicking as pretence to please Charlie Faber Monteith. I would strongly suggest that H's verse, if it shows anything in *North* proves his boredom with the North of Ireland which was a feature of middle-class Ireland in the South, well before 1975. H had absconded from NI like a scared rat. Middle class Southern Ireland squealed like scared rats anytime the North seemed closer to them.

"Act of Union" attempts a hold-all of Irish history, but as you can imagine if you've never read it, the gaps are disgracefully glaring for an ordinary published writer like H. All he can posit is that 'Conquest is a lie' (NSP 66-87; 74). This is Undergraduate history. Johnston finds that 'Heaney's metaphors — gourd and prune — abet the bog in metamorphosing the girl from a human state' (IPAJ 149). Johnston, of course finds everything 'metaphorically rich' (IPAJ 149). Those who find a nod to Yeats's "Leda and the Swan" are way off. England is a ram and Ireland 'the stretchmarked body'[...] like opened ground' (NSP 66-87; 75). What is obscene is the acquiescent hint in the use of 'No treaty/I foresee will salve completely' (NSP 66-87; 75).

And this became a trademark of his which he re-used in "Hercules and Antaeus" representing his feeble grasp of Irish history. Behind all of this, is academic verse at its worst, the maker flicking through anthologies and creative writing anthologies of poetry, desperately seeking a few kick-starts for the farce of his verse. The results are well described in the colloquial: what you get is arsy-versy and H licking up to Charlie Faber. H is indistinguishable between arse and elbow in his verse. Hercules is given the verbal clinker and assonance 'snake-choker, dung heaver' (NSP 66-87; 76) which is kids verse with plenty of noisy words that amount to jabberwocky. No sentience, no interest except obviously to H whose main task was to feed the Faberman a farmyard yield in versicles. Antaeus is, as you might guess (if you have got the hang of H's diction) 'the mould-hugger' (NSP 66-87; 76). Of course, he is. And Hercules as in child's verse: 'lifts his arms/in a remorseless V' (NSP 66-87; 77). Don't go looking for a modernist gloss in H from Ovid or any classical poet. H is just not competent enough to get beyond a derivative Hopkinesque wordscape but without any recognition of Hopkins's struggles in terms of gender, theology and the office of poetry.

So what are H's politics? Well, they are smug, snug, and squat in "Whatever You Say Say Nothing". This diction might have been a better path for him, but he couldn't pursue it. Besides it proves my point about H as scared escapee from the boredom of the black North and its war. Thus, his deliberate posing as an exile while being middle-class safely away in Wicklow: no bombs, no bullets, no sectarian murders, no 'gelignite and sten' as he puts it (NSP 66-87; 78). The problem here is the internal journalese which is all you get. The piece might well be one of those fillers in Sunday journalism for the lazy reader on Mainland Britain who wants reassurance that the North of Ireland is far off, heavily policed, and militarily contained, if imperially annexed by the UK. So, that when H claims: 'Of the "wee six" I sing' (NSP 66-87; 79) this is the real presumption, the real fakery because unlike balladeers and songsters of the era, he did not sing about the Six Counties. You realise that he is totally in absence, as he finds both communities conveniently for him 'Besieged within the siege' (NSP 66-87; 80). H is singing for Charlie and Britain. H loathed the Six Counties like his bosom buddy Cruise O'Brien the great humbug and phoney historian.

1970-71. However, the west coast and its vibrant poetries could not dampen his Irish bogland-farmyard anecdotes that had to be pushed into a mush of Jutland mythology.

Harvard was to beckon in 1981 for a long stint until 1996, until he dropped out as Boylston Professorship for Emerson Poet in Residence in sunny Cambridge, Massachusetts. In between, the Nobel committee had received his CV backdrop, based on the Faber & Faber caché, amidst the posse of professors who vouched for H as a real poet, presented as International and Tabloid safe 'news' since he was a conservative post-hippy academic domiciled in Southern Ireland and silent without any anti-British viewpoint.

"Oysters" is comfortable escapist verse rather than mention Belfast or Derry, for H on holidays in Italy is drinking wine and eating oysters, with basic data from the Guidebook about the Romans: yes, actually the Romans ate oysters. Gosh, never knew that 'til I read H. H wants the tang of the oyster to 'quicken me all into verb, pure verb' (NSP 66-87; 92). O be gob, he feels a verse coming up from his oyster-laden guts. H doesn't say which verb. "Triptych" is three pieces (!) the first "After a Killing" but expectations are soon displaced when rural life emerges with a four line closing description of a girl carrying a basket of vegetables: 'With the tops and mould still fresh on them' (NSP 66-87; 93). Well, if you dig fresh vegetables what do you expect: to have them already washed by Tesco? "The Toome Road" has a tiny hint of the NI war with British troops who pass him along the road. His reaction is extraordinary in its romanticism:

O charioteers, above your dormant guns,

It stands here still, stands vibrant as you pass,

The invisible, untoppled omphalos (NSP 66-87; 96).

His pump against their imperialism. Hey, what a rebel. H's feeble triumphalism over the Queen's Highway which is the bogus claim of Loyalist settlers but there is no actual history in "The Toome Road". The extent of the NI war, of course meant that everyone was touched by sectarian deaths. So H too has an elegy for his cousin, Colum McCartney in "The Strand at Lough Beg". It is delicate to write criticism in such circumstances. In other words, weighing aesthetic considerations above carnage and murder, but H's verse is immune, as it both directs itself specifically and yet remains outside and impervious. The event of this man's murder was a quotidian happening, and such circumstances had repetitious features increasing the monstrosity, grotesqueness and evil of such killings. H does at least bring in the night drive fears (for once) showing his own plight:

Or in your driving mirror, tailing headlights

That pulled out suddenly and flagged you down (NSP 66-87; 98).

One just about glimpses the horrors that were present with gangs of paramilitaries manning roadways, lawless, and drunk, ready to dispense their brand of Loyalist murder. Instead of dealing directly with what happened, H imagines Colum re-appearing: 'With blood and roadside muck in your hair and eyes' (NSP 66-87; 99). The method and the glimpse and the imprecision, render the murder at a very low threshold, as you have to grasp at what little is given in his attempt at universalising random roadside murders in the dark of night, and he fails. It is less than bad journalism. In every sense the elegy is unstated and vague.

As you turn the page, you feel that with "Casualty" the North's war never invaded his subject matter or content. There are hints at the and the artist releasing it. H, of course misheard it, or misread it, and gets it woefully wrong, appropriating it from Oisin Kelly, the Irish sculpture 'as if the grain/Remembered what the mallet used to know' (NSP 66-87; 110). H repeats his obsequious metaphor about verse being like opened ground (which it is not, never was, never is) and concludes 'Each verse returning like the plough turned round' (NSP 66-87; 110). It's an aimless sequence of ten 'sonnets' to fill up *Field Work* and mark Saddlemyer, and her granting H the gate-lodge. As verse to a patron in responses of gratitude, it follows such weaker performances about deliberately composing to a purpose. The sequence has a notoriously nervous attempt at the erotic in its conclusion. Copulation is described as 'the lovely and painful/Covenants of flesh' (NSP 66-87; 118). Were they flailing each other naked with sods of turf or what? Or digging with spades—naked in the moonlight! In every respect contact with H's verse is an experience of absurdity, ludicrousness and ridicule upon himself.

In *Field Work* there is a Dantescan interlude from the *Inferno*. Dante must have seemed so inexpert to H. Dante with no farmyards of souls, or turf burning cookers in hell. Ugolino starving to death with his sons who have been bricked up in a tower during conflict, well known to aficionados' of Dante. H plumps for the most obvious violent episode in the *Inferno*. Johnston finds redolence in this based on H's own statement:

> I sensed there was something intimate, almost carnal, about those feuds and sorrows of medieval Pisa, something that could perhaps mesh and house the equivalent and destructive energies in, say, contemporary Belfast (IPAJ 157-8).

So he pretends to link thirteenth century Pisa with contemporary Belfast—you can hear the nervous fake voice trying it on, and hoping to get away with it. Belfast is Hell, Dante wrote about Hell. Hey, why don't I get a sexy chunk of Dante that can be implied to reference Belfast, which I am told by the newspapers, is Hell. Good idea. 'I translated "Ugolino" in order for it to be read in the context of the "dirty protests" in the Maze prison' (StSt, 425). This is H's shamefaced implication. Well, you need a big gesture to abuse incarcerated suffering Republican prisoners, and obviously go for a top brand name: Dante.

"An Afterwards" is H dabbling with Dante again, a feature of his life with Faber whose stalwart T. S. Eliot re-invented the Dantescan mode among other modernists. For H to string along with this was a definite displacement and to anyone who knows Dante, realises its usage by H is posturing. Here, H's wife has complained about the absences in the domestic scene with H locked in his study. The wife is quoted as wanting 'all poets in the ninth circle'. Wow, this is highly Dantescan, isn't it? Oh, very clever. Again the exchange is egotistical and seeing as the charge against him is 'the sulphurous news of poets and poetry' (NSP 66-87; 119). As wit it's weak. As a report on the domestic scene, it is silent. The punishment she wishes to inflict on him is 'A rabid egotistical daisy-chain' (NSP 66-87; 119) which is peculiarly weird. A real woman would not be so tame, flowery, or sham poetical.

Meanwhile "The Otter" can be consigned to his animal pieces. They are usually forbidding and this one no less. The scene is Tuscany. The otter is having a swim which is described, then he emerges from the water

frisky in your freshened pelt,

Printing the stones' (NSP 66-87; 121).

This conclusion is meant to be his verse's *coup de grace* as you have to think: 'Printing'? Get it, the water hits the stones, and the otter is kind of an ink colour, if you push yourself far enough to accept this, the wet stones kinda look like he's printing them. Or something like that. You can see how awkward it is as a metaphor.

Next it's "The Skunk" echoing Lowell's method in "Skunk Hour". H's skunk reminds him of a priest 'damasked like the chasuble/At a funeral mass' (NSP 66-87; 122) the reference is Catholic, if you don't get it; but why push this as a valid metaphor except that he has a canny purpose as will be revealed in the last line. H is in California, the wife is away, so it's a love poem and the skunk brings her to mind. How she can be a skunk: it might be mildly erotic but let's hope she doesn't smell like a skunk? H tells this as a memory-piece:

By the sootfall of your things at bedtime,

Your head down, tail-up hunt in a bottom drawer

For the black plunge-line nightdress (NSP 66-87; 122).

Let's face it: this hint of erotica is laboured. Can a woman evoked as a skunk, really be a turn on? Hey, I have to hurry home to the skunk tonight. H's sootfall evokes nausea. She is not even engaged with sexual activity but naked and fumbling about in the bottom drawer, and if so, why bother for the cliché-cold imagery of 'plunge-line nightdress'. The sexuality is dull, giving the impression of a domestic rather than a sexually charged atmosphere. One cannot identify with this sort of stilted voyeurism that suggests the sorting of clothes amidst banal conversation. Who thinks about a skunk at such a time? H's sexuality is not asserted and comes across as dormant.

"A Dream of Jealousy" might spice things up a bit but is meant, or purports to the following. H, his wife, and another woman are walking 'In wooded parkland' (NSP 66-87; 123) (yes, it's a yawning description) when they sit on the grass for a picnic. It gets worse. H admits in front of his wife to the other woman 'I have much coveted, your breast's mauve star' (NSP 66-87; 123). It's a mealy-mouthed request, and according to the anecdote the other woman flashed her breasts, and Mrs H had a 'wounded stare' (NSP 66-87; 123). "Song" in the collection *Field Work* is an unacknowledged quote from an ancient Celtic poem where he lifts the closing line 'the music of what happens' (NSP 66-87; 127) without acknowledging the source of his best and borrowed line translated from the ancient Gaelic.

"The Harvest Bow" proves that such material could have been used better, but of course real nature poets can, but not H. What is the meaning of 'your fingers moved somnambulant' (NSP 66-87; 128). 'I tell and finger it like braille' (NSP 66-87; 128) this is the fabric of the harvest bow quite a common sight in rural houses. Here you see H making it folksy and back-to-nature, he reflects in lazy nostalgia. 'And if I spy into its golden loops' (NSP 66-87; 128). To read his so called nature verse is like a Wikipedia of detail, sporadic, and vacuous, as well as hit and miss.

H desecrates the farming world which he plunders for material. The harvest bow pinned up on the dresser renders his usual folksy feel, and he uses italics to swagger the line '*The end of art is peace*' (NSP 66-87; 129). "In Memoriam Francis Ledwidge" forms part of the World War I fake-commemorative verse as hagiography: 'I think of you in your Tommy's uniform,/A haunted Catholic face, pallid and brave' (NSP 66-87; 131). Look at it: the insincerity of the lines. H is using a famous poet to hang his pallid lines upon, a soldier who died in the disgusting evil of WWI. H insists on posing as if he knows every iota of Ledwidge. It is flagrantly abusive, this sort of verse in its shameful little quatrains, eked out to please the Fabermen. For a finish, he attempts a historical insert, but all of H's history is potted and clichéd 'In you, our dead enigma' (NSP 66-87; 131). This conclusion is a vulgar assumption that the soldiers of the North of Ireland found a unity in sectarianism 'all of you consort now underground' (NSP 66-87; 131). Henry Hart is woefully misguided in comparing H's verse on Ledwidge to Lowell's "For the Union Dead": 'the political and religious tergiversation that appeared in the Lowell elegy reappears in the elegy to Francis Ledwidge' (Hart 127). There is no religious statement in either poem and Hart uses a whooper of a word in 'tergiversation' but such is the majority of academic woolly writing as some sort of mystique and fraudulence. Tergiversation is a useful definition of such writing that is evasive and ambiguous.

H actually misses Ledwidge's wartorn conscience totally. Ledwidge 'deserted' and went to Dublin in 1916 and hoped to join the Irish Volunteers and Irish Citizen Army but in his British uniform was unable logistically to enter the fray with Pearse and Connolly. Instead, he returned to Ebrington Barracks, Derry where he was jailed and then released into the trenches of WWI—a Royal family feud-war requiring slaughter for four years.

H's "Sweeney Astray" I abhor, simply because it has far more able translators. What goes against his ability to achieve it, is his lack of disturbance or poetic frenzy, or a poet's mental instability. As in the title piece, marred by being banal:

in cold Glenelly,

flocks of birds quickly

coming and going (NSP 66-87; 136)

'Sweeney' demands an English version that registers the extremity of poetry, its intensity and the beauty of fragility. H had none of these gifts. Sweeney has lists, since the Gaelic verse from this era utilised such, but this is lost on H who makes the litanies pedestrian. Place-names in Sweeney are part of the word-magic but with H you feel you are reading a road map, aimlessly. Sweeney as Irish King Lear is not visible, audible, or present in H's version, just as the profound breakdown of the subject as flailed poet, is never apparent. H's botched effort does not merit a close reading.

The only use of 'disturbed' in H is the ineptness of "Sloe Gin" where this appears as his typical mish-mash of description and hyperbole:

When I unscrewed it

I smelled the disturbed

tart stillness of a bush

rising through the pantry (NSP 66-87; 147).

No, he doesn't mean a disturbed tart or any slang. In Academic parlance this 'expresses the thoughts of a speaker prompted by drinking his glass of sloe gin' (*Pop Can* 266). Danson Brown does not articulate beyond saying 'Heaney is a Faber poet, publishing in "London", marketed to a broad range of English-speaking readers' (*Pop Can* 276). Marketed is the correct word alright—hence H and the great poetry hoax.

"Sandstone Keepsake" is a good example of the over-described opening:

It is a kind of chalky russet

solidified gourd, sedimentary

and so reliably dense and bricky

I often clasp it and throw if from hand to hand (NSP 66-87; 150).

This is appalling as a chunk of imprecision and as an opening gambit, leaves one exhausted with the attempt at reading the jerky efforts at precise description. Guy de Montfort from the *Inferno* suddenly pops into the lines which is further Dantescan posturing. In other words, a red stone easily fits H's internal reference metaphor machinery, and makes no sense as to why the stone should call up one of the damned from the *Inferno*. The fakery here is that H is so familiar with Dante that immediately any red stone evokes Phlegethon, and has him musing as to whether the stone was 'bloodied on the bed of hell's hot river?'(NSP 66-87; 150) No, no, no. Rocks and stones are not from Hell. Nor is there any such thing as a stone available from Dante's great poem which is made out of words, not stones. You cannot find an actual stone in any poem. It makes one wonder is H a simpleton or a lunatic. No, he's actually not that complex. It's hoodwinking and fooling, or attempting to fool the unwary while his smug supporters like Monteith needed to cultivate the farmyard golden goose H.

"Station Island" is a sequence I-XII and challenging as to its comprehension, because of H's imprecision and inaccuracies, as well as the failure of the visionary facility. H is on St Patrick's Purgatory in County Donegal, and first off meeting the ghost of William Carleton, the novelist famous for his literature of the Irish divide, especially his novel of the Famine *The Black Prophet*. H's cardboard-Carleton is presented in a travesty within the usual excessive reflex of lines like 'I who learned to read in the reek of flax' (NSP 66-87; 167). H parallels himself with Carleton's era which is short-handing the history, and here you find the whole germ of the idea for the sequence in that Carleton (1794-1869) wrote a short story *Lough Derg Pilgrim*. H takes it as license to blunder into concocting an Irish *purgatorio* already far better 'done' by Denis Devlin and Patrick Kavanagh. Carleton in H's narration, joins him in the car and H admits 'The angry role was never my vocation' (NSP 66-87; 167) this is again absconding from the NI War. Carleton's conclusion of the centuries long Plantation-Sectarian-War is highly trite as presumed in H's voice-over for the novelist:

We are earthworms of the earth, and all that

has gone through us is what will be our trace (NSP 66-87; 168).

Anyone writing 'we are earthworms of the earth' is being lazy while unable to recognise that repetition of the word 'earth' is weak, whatever about the turgid use of 'earthworms' borrowed and badly from Shakespeare. Normally, people just say and write 'worms' not 'earthworms'; the earth part is a given. But I need to re-iterate that H is a dangerous user of language because a mis-user and usually for his guttural affectation problem. A sloppy user of language will never be considered a poet. A real poet's use of language exhibits one of the excellences of the art form.

Next up, is the unnamed priest from the foreign missions. In every respect, a figure saturated within Irish literature, and H's version in the light of contemporary Ireland makes his portrait very jaded and bygone. The priest is compared to a bicycle, no symbolism implied presumably

His name had lain undisturbed for years

like an old bicycle wheel in a ditch

ripped at last from under jungling briars (NSP 66-87; 171).

This is useless as an image, and cannot equate to any person. It is a misuse of the Dantescan element that entered poetry through Eliot, principally in *Little Gidding*. H's 'notes' are sparse on Carleton, Kavanagh and St John of the Cross. Besides the supernatural is debunked as the priest queries H: 'What are you doing, going through the motions?' This renders the pilgrim redundant as an agnostic. H is easily seen through, as using this meta-literary device for his fake Dantecan usage.

Eliot's ghostly figure in *Little Gidding* has originality, it startles as a new method, even if not as visionary as Dante's, but behind it and around it, is the monumental religious quest of the poet already steeped in various traditions which grants high validity to *Four Quartets* and its closing section in *Little Gidding*. H is miserably attempting Eliot's method. H's so-called ghosts in *Station Island* are hollow. In part v meeting an old schoolmaster named Murphy, the poetic principle is quoted but in italics, spoiling the ghostly voice, as if italics could authenticate the format '*For what is the great/moving power and spring of verse? Feeling, and/in particular, love*' (NSP 66-87; 175).

The great moving power of verse, among other qualities to make it so, are not evident in H's great verse hoax. Instead, you get in abundance what is given a few lines down

When you're on the road

give lifts to people, you'll always learn something.

This is laughable and contradictory, and mocking of Carleton who is given a lift by the narrator, but there is nothing to learn from H, except perhaps through outing his admirers.

Section vii has a 'ghost' from the Sectarian War, the victim of a night-hit by two gunmen. At once this character, a cousin of H's has had his forehead 'blown open above the eye and blood/had dried on his neck and cheek' (NSP 66-87; 179). This is not Dantescan, but Dell comic status. Furthermore the 'dead' one says: 'it's only me. You've seen men as raw/after a football match' (NSP 66-87; 179). These colloquial, demotic intrusions and juxtapositions greatly lessen any intended impact. The night raid that involves a murder is graphic novel standard, and with it H intrudes to centre himself in his continual front-man position of defending his non-position on the sectarian NI War:

Forgive the way I lived indifferent—

forgive my timid circumspect involvement (NSP 66-87; 182).

Weak and all as this is, he becomes narcissistic: 'I surprised myself' (NSP 66-87; 182) the admission is a staged implication, and that he would admit this by printing it through Faber and Faber. H cannot reach the excellence of Dante's dialogue method from the *Inferno* as Eliot's smirched head-on with the ghost that just about works in *Little Gidding*. The pleading of H's 'dead' cousin is utterly unconvincing and given the *bon-mot* oft used by H re-using his birthday 13th April, when Colum says 'Ah poet, lucky poet, tell me why' (NSP 66-87; 184). Colum literally struck down, laments this fact, and H's metaphysics are incorrect. 'And so I pleaded with my second cousin' (NSP 66-87; 185). None of the imagery is remarkable. Colum accuses him:

the way you whitewashed ugliness and drew

the lovely blinds of the *Purgatorio*

and saccharined my death with morning dew (NSP 66-87; 185).

Again this doublethink does not fool me, as H the cutehoor verse-maker has no artistic presence to re-make a *Purgatorio* out of this material which is serious but merely hints a sectarian murder. It is a cash-in and a cop out on H's part. Resolutions are sentimental as section ix closes:

Then I thought of the tribe whose dances never fail

For they keep dancing till they sight the deer (NSP 66-87; 188).

What does this mean? Nothing. It is primarily faulty pseudo-imitation of early Yeats. Pilgrimages conclude with seeking the self, forgiveness, and ultimate vision but here the monk says:

Read poems as prayers [...] and for your penance

translate me something by Juan de la Cruz (NSP 66-87; 190).

This is of course vacuous, very forced, and very unconvincing.

There is a set piece with a refrain in xi that goes 'although it is the night' which is actually irritating through repetition (NSP 66-87; 191). Finally, in xii, H meets James Joyce, of all people, making Station Island a kind of literary chat show with the imaginary glittering guest list. H, is of course super-serious about meeting Joyce as the stilted language reveals. The rhetoric is inches thick, when JJ tells him 'What you do you must do on your own' (NSP 66-87; 192) and other sundry creative writing workshop utterances, all in pretence of the voice of Joyce 'The main thing is to write/for the joy of it' (NSP 66-87; 192).This is so basic as to amount to a printed recipe for instant embarrassment. The problem here is that Joyce would never utter such rubbish. A major stylist like Joyce would also not use garbled syntax: 'what you do you must do on your own' is a convoluted piece of rhetorical illogicality. It is actually meaningless like all rhetoric. It is showy, egotistical and fake. Joyce never said any such thing to H. H invented this jumble of words. In fact, had H quoted accurately something Joyce actually said about writing, the verse might have been the better for it. However, nothing can save H's verse.

"In the Beech" begins 'I was a lookout posted and forgotten' (NSP 66-87; 194) yet another childhood anecdote, guessable from the start about going alone to a tree as primeval experience where it became 'My tree of knowledge' (NSP 66-87; 194). "The First Kingdom" displays this sort of recalled pseudo-birth of the verse-maker extraordinaire, pushed into bravado and braggadocio: all that is required are the opening lines to prove my point:

The royal roads were cow paths.

The queen mother hunkered on a stool

and played the harpstrings of milk

into a wooden pail (NSP 66-87; 195).

This is borrowed from Kavanagh's "A Christmas Childhood" without the emotional immediacy. H's detritus, posing as Parnassian utterance is derivative: imposing this on students and young people is a waste of their time. How could anyone see the metaphor of milking a cow with playing the harp: it is forced gross nonsense. Besides milking is a delicate skill, any clumsy gestures can cause mastitis to the cow's teats but H's milking is like all of his rural life, feeble and fictional.

"The First Flight" is also in this vein with H 'relearning/the acoustic of frost//and the meaning of woodnote' (NSP 66-87; 196). "The Cleric" has more of the same: 'I heard new words prayed at cows/in the byre' (NSP 66-87; 200). The rest you can guess. "The Master" 'He dwelt in himself/like a rook in an unroofed tower' (NSP 66-87; 202). Yes, what a clanger, what an insult to the glory of God and all rooks in their glory and beauty. "In Tempore" are Catholic recollections of having a Mass prayer book which is described where 'the word rubric itself a bloodshot sunset' (NSP 66-87; 206). Here is H's aberration, that a writer of verse is all day long, seeing one thing as something else, so his prayer book causes the hallucination of a sunset, but there is neither prayer book nor sunset conveyed in the lines. H has no acquaintance with genuine hallucination either, and all his attempts to render such are laughable.

"Alphabets" is similar memory stuff about schooldays:

'Smells of inkwells rise in the classroom hush.

A globe in the window tilts like a coloured O' (NSP 66-87; 211).

How can this be classified as anything but a weak metaphor, and the only thing a globe suggests is an 'O'. "Alphabets" fast-forwards through schooldays and re-uses the globe introducing

The astronaut sees all he has sprung from,

The risen, aqueous, singular, lucent O

Like a magnified and buoyant ovum—(NSP 66-87; 213).

It's frighteningly simplistic, a kind of make-up-a-verse by describing a globe on a school window. Describe the globe as an 'O' and then add in the astronaut. O, and name the poem "Alphabets". "Terminus" pushes childhood further into preciousness with H's: 'Two buckets were easier carried than one./I grew up in between' (NSP 66-87; 214). It is awful, sentimental, dreary, and of no merit.

"From the Frontier of Writing" is a transparent example of how H merges two themes in his fake-a-verse, fix-a-verse, concoct-a-verse methodology by fusing together a dash of false profundity with a bit of scenery but there is intrinsically no direct link between the two parts. The scene is an army checkpoint, wellknown in NI; this one is manned by British Troops (so far everything is quite journalese and obvious) and H senses 'that quiver in the self' (NSP 66-87; 216).

The checkpoint becomes a metaphor for writing, yes, he was stuck with the checkpoint thing and thought, wait now, a tweak here and tweak there, and hey presto: crossing through a checkpoint becomes the writing of verse. Get it? Frankly, no. Crossing through a checkpoint may result in a poem but writing a poem is not the equivalent of going through a British army checkpoint as described by H. You cannot describe or evoke the writing of a poem. The writing of a poem is in the written poem: it is the poem itself. Yes, there is the genre of *ars poeticae* poems but H's version is not one of these. I fail this one as trying to fool some sort of reader into believing that this poem is about poetry writing. The metaphors are thick; passing through the checkpoint is like having 'passed from behind a waterfall' (NSP 66-87; 216). Again his fake surrealism and invented hallucinations.

"The Haw Lantern" represents him in typical performance, melodramatic, hyperbolic, metaphorical and inaccurate 'a small light for small people' is the fairylore mentioned while in the second stanza, the haw lantern is the dangling red berry and morphs into Diogenes 'seeking one just man'; so the reader is getting a smattering of Wikipedia knowledge. Then, it animates as if the haw lantern has H 'scrutinized'. The haw bush does not look at people, come on. The red berry of the haw is described:

its blood-prick that you wish would test you and clear you,

its pecked-at ripeness that scans you, then moves on (NSP 66-87; 217).

Factually, the haw lantern does not exist. H's admirers did not realise that there is no such thing as a haw lantern? Diogenes held an actual lantern in daylight on his tirades around Rome not a haw berry on a twig. The drawing on the collection of that name by Carol Wilhide does not resemble the red berry on the hawthorn bush which is spherical like a bead. Wilhide's berry is a rosehip which is distinctly ovoid in shape. Anyway, people in the countryside know the difference but H is invariably wrong in his nature notes, country people in County Derry and County Donegal say 'the hawthorn' not 'the haw'. Faber were obviously none too bothered to verify what kind of berry H meant, perhaps trusting their farmyard guru to know his berries.

"From the Republic of Conscience" is a fantasia of sorts; you have to say kind of, because it lacks political content, if you consider the year of publication: 1987. Thus lines like 'your symptoms of creeping privilege disappeared' (NSP 66-87; 218) are trivial as with

all life sprang

from salt in tears which the sky-god wept (NSP 66-87; 219).

It's frighteningly bad. So arch, so obtuse, so full of verbal looseness.

Examine "The Stone Verdict" 'where the stones were verdicts'[...] 'Until he stood waist deep in the cairn' (NSP 66-87; 222) and this has the same ending as "The Haw Lantern" that stone will judge H's verse. Neither stones nor haw lanterns can read. The Mammy poem is no 3 in "Clearances" with the awkward inane metaphor is the apotheosis of sentimentality with son and mother beyond credulity that this is the only moment of their lives when they were close:

When all the others were away at Mass

I was all hers as we peeled potatoes.

They broke the silence, let fall one by one (NSP 66-87; 227).

It's ridiculous and is there a metaphor? Of course: 'Like solder weeping off the soldering iron' (NSP 66-87; 227). So, in one line you get the potatoes, and soon you are into the soldering iron because H's imaginative powers cannot think of anything else on the spur of the moment. Charlie Monteith is waiting for the next collection. H is teaching and teaching, and has little time to versify, so he has to write fast, hence you get the concatenation of potato and weeping solder from the soldering iron. Did you not know that all soldering irons weep? H believed that they weep. No 5 in the sequence has a comment about drying clothes that is H's mark of stupidity:

The cool that came off sheets just off the line

Made me think the damp must still be in them (NSP 66-87; 229)

It is a very simple process. Sheets are washed, they are hung out to dry and can be damp on being taken off the line. The secret is to try and dry them in good weather, or better still there are such things as clothes dryers. Incredible observation by H: so incredible that people who have to do the washing, unlike H, hardly notice the power of dampness they get used to it. "The Milk Factory" presents a personification that is ludicrous:

There we go, soft-eyed calves of the dew,

Astonished and assumed into flourescence' (NSP 66-87; 233).

It is very difficult to read his verse without emotions of exasperation, frustration, and astonishment at the ludicrous stupidity.

V: Heaney's translation disasters and bloopers

H's presumption as translator emerged with the 'burn-out' from farmland themes and Faber & Faber's demands for successive collections. So, H shifted wearily, I might add, towards Dante, and later his version of *Beowulf*. What stings the ear about H as translator is that H is always plodding along awkwardly in the language: 'Hidden in the thick of a tree is a bough made of gold' (ST 3). Many lines are in this diction and the subject is obviously "The Golden Bough" a translation from Virgil, *Aeneid*, VI (ST 1) or this one: 'And the foliage growing upon it glimmers the same' (ST 1). Even this extract is damning in terms of limp diction, there is simply no majesty, no ascent into a H-voice that might make him a translator of skill.

Kirchway thinks differently, but Kirch is a guy making good bucks out of a literature career in BU, so he gotta toe the H-line:

> With characteristic brilliance, Heaney refuses to let words and images not earn their keep'. '*Discordia demens,* for example, becomes the headline-worthy "fanatical violence." Others he achieves through the imagination and the ear. Charon, who ferries the souls of the dead, is "bearded with unclean white shag" in a world of "congregating dark" where the three-headed dog of hell is pacified with a "dumpling of soporific honey," and the guilty are punished in Tartarus to the sound of "the fling and scringe and drag / Of iron chains." A helmsman cast adrift remarks that "a south wind / Hurled me and burled me," and the sea's surface is "molten marble." When Aeneas says to the Sibyl, "I have foreseen / And foresuffered all," it might be argued that Heaney is hewing a bit too close to Eliot's Tiresias in "The Waste Land," but there is pleasure even in this literary nod. (Kirchway NY Times 20).

Not close to Eliot, rather closer to *Batman* the TV series with visual stills of noisy words filling the screen during fight scenes.

Batman TV Series screen still images reflecting H's noisy guttural language usage.

H's *Beowulf* resides as a self-admiring reproduction. The language register is too mixed for its own good. H insists on 'dialect', in point of fact, he has to make pretence to dialect, that is what is expected, so he is using 'thole' and words such as 'bothies' 'God-given' and rendering Beowulf as 'Beow'. The name in the original text is Bēowulf, son of Scyldes and the reader learns that Bēowulf is what modern parlance would call a pet-name. If H had 'done' Homer, the diminutive form might well have appeared 'Uly' for Ulysses, 'Hect' for Hector, and Achilles in the truly Irish rendering as 'Achill'. The double ridicule on H is that repression decreased his flawed writing further: making contemporary Ulster of no interest, until he could bash about noisily and fake-up Beowulf into an Ulster-Oirish story. It isn't an Ulster story. It is pre-middle ages Norse. And it is too adjectival for its own good, as H fell for the lure of gutturals.

H makes much in beginning his flights of verse paragraphs with 'So', and the overuse elsewhere of 'So', as if he had invented a new form of 'Once upon a time' opening. There is a surfeit of words in the obvious transitions: 'Then as dawn brightened and the day broke' (B 6). Dawn brightening ensures daybreak; there is no need to mention day. Incidentally, H's Beowulf hasn't the ghost of a chance of echoing the original. The hallmark of translation is that it gives echoes of the original. H is echoless:

On a height they kindled the hugest of all

funeral pyres (B 98).

He nearly went 'for the mother of all funeral pyres' and the use of 'hugest' is really clumsy. Just as I object to his use of 'the hall of halls' (B 5). The line and a half is illustrative of bad handling in a bad version making the use of mere 'height' very weak. A few lines on you get 'wailed aloud' (B 98). A crowd in grief can be loud in their wailing. There is much of this obfuscation and glutting. Behind the whole project is, of course *Beowulf* for the Old English and Anglo-Saxon college curricula with Faber & Faber cashing in, and using their mascot H. It's like *Coca Cola* has another product after *Zero*, it is H's *Beowulf* read the label: contains sugary language, thick globs of adjectives and stale lines.

From the artistic point of view, H is continually mealy-mouthed, and by this does a disservice to modern versions which forces innocent readers towards his Faber prescribed dosage of verbiage. Modern translation has traditions beginning with the Poundian syntax of "The Seafarer" and Canto I, and on through Lowell and Rexroth. H demotes *Beowulf* which has had a few real poet translators, and plain prose versions. H and Beowulf are an unwieldy mix of show-off in ugly language. The lure of 'a local Ulster word' (B xxix) seemed 'to have special body and force' (B xxx) hence his justification in using 'graith' for 'harness' and 'hoked' for 'rooted about'. Who actually needs another layer of verbiage, reaching back to any other linguistic register. H's folkloric localism is really trying. The student will of course have to endure his introduction to the poem, and comment on the use of Ulsteristics, *but please do not mention that distressing Sectarian War.*

Beowulf has been rendered into modern English through Anglo-Saxon idioms, and at that, removed from its source which is ancient Norseland, modern Scandinavia. H's version is based on C. L. Wrenn with H's original ponderousness added. The Anglo-Saxon dialect of Beowulf, finally written down around 1000A.D. is not a harsh guttural tongue, as in the following sample *geseah stēapne hrōf golde fāhne* literally 'he saw the roof was adorned in gold'. I stay by my own happy enough meetings with the poem. It is best in a homogenous version, even a rigorous biblical version, in keeping with an adapted biblical style would standardise the experience, rather than H's dabbling with words and bits of phrases beloved of his farmyard. Pound took on a selected sequence from the 'Nekuia' Odyssey XI for his opening Canto. He had the artistic grace to insert it as the acknowledged 'lift' from Andreas Divus version of 1538. I can admire the Poundian method which bore fruit and presaged his own life journey. As a poet full of prescriptions in aesthetics, he states 'we test a translation by the feel, and particularly by the feel of being in contact with the force of a great original' (EPLE 271).

The real problem with H is that one is aware of so much striving and discord to present Beowulf as something he wrote himself. This leads to that over-used cliché of praise in twentieth century poetry after Pound, where translations are applauded by academic critics saying 'H has actually produced a whole new poem in translation, nothing lost, nothing awkward in fact a new addition to literature'. Pound never felt like this, and this is what makes the difference. H pompously assures the student-reader that here is a translation, here is *Beowulf* because here is H who translated it. And the Faber wrapper for the indoctrinated academic consumer.

H makes great claims for comprehending how 'uisce' and the 'River Usk' morphed into whiskey. Is this meant to be his license to presume that translation is easy and authentic, a mere linguistic trick, and there you are reading Norse through a perfect glaze of twentieth century Heaneyisms. Such linguistic boasts in the Introduction move on to citing the Anglo-Saxon Þolian meaning 'to suffer' as he ecstatically recalls his aunt's ergot: '"They'll just have to learn to thole", my aunt would say about some family who had suffered an unforeseen bereavement' (B xxv). This leads to the realisation that 'my aunt's language was not just a self-enclosed family possession but an historical heritage' (B xxv).

His aunt could have done a better version of Beowulf if she had the time, is his woefully ignorant remark in not understanding which he must have, that Norse is not English nor could one line in either language reach the actuality of tone, rhythm, speech, sound and diction of the original language. Thus H is thinking that adopting an archaic word based on the Anglo-Saxon Þolian grants him the license to presume. All based on one word. It is disgusting in its deceit, in dealing with language as it if it were glue that you use to stick letters of the alphabet together. H makes Beowulf into a shapeless Lego construction that falls over.

Despite all his family heirloom linguistics and protestations, H is ever dislocated in phraseology in Beowulf, such as 'Retainers in great numbers/were posted on guard as so often in the past' (B 41). The effect is of hearing the creak of Wrenn's glossary amidst H's creaking forward with another line from his own English usage, and the affectation of piling on the dialect where possible as if that will somehow render the epic poem into some presentable version, fooling the reader with archaic words by positing them close to Norse. It is what Americans call: bullshit. H insists on making something that might look like Anglo-Saxon-Scandinavian-Ulster Scotch invented speech which is why his version reads like something from the planet Beowulf.

Beowulf speaks thus: 'Wise sir, do not grieve' (B 46). It's like Hamlet, as if re-drafted by Larry Olivier while drunk. 'The iron blade with its ill-boding patterns' (B 48). The many sword references are lugubrious, set in H's lines out of desperation to pour the translation into some fitting mould. H also misses the armoury-content, the presence of weapons in this warlike tableaux and his renderings of Scandinavian psychology are pre-Freudian: 'his life lost happiness' (B 56). Faced with what the hero has to do and achieve, he had recourse to various moods which make a laugh of the psychology:

Go on dear Beowulf, do everything

you said you would when you were still young (B 84).

The acknowledgments to H's translation reveal the scholarly mercantilism of the trade college edition, planned originally by Norton and Norton at the behest of M. H. Abrams and Jon Stallworthy, and through Faber's bright old boy, Christopher Reid as well as Paul Keegan whose tastes are those of the bully. Professor Greenblatt of HU, and of course the prioress of Harvard Yard herself, Helena the Vendor, are barely glossed in, as is the able Professor of HU, William Alfred. Precedence reigns in academia. The lunatics run the asylum. Alfred translated Beowulf but many do, and have done. Faber wanted the academic market share; aesthetics, translation and such matters were secondary.

H's involvement with the Kochanowski's *Laments* is a different matter, as he admitted he was not translating, but 'revising another person's work' (Laments 11). Stanislaw Bananczak had already rendered the Polish-Slavic original into modern English, albeit adhering to strict rhyming couplets. To judge this, as H's translation mode is inaccurate. H was really proof-reader, making some additions and suggestions. I reviewed the Kochanowski put out by Gallery and don't intend to quote myself.

I am not going to waste as much space and time on H's Sophocles as I gave to Beowulf. I laugh indeed at the phrase: H's Sophocles. He went for the obvious, thus naming it *The Burial at Thebes* and basically the whole set-up was an Abbey Theatre, Dublin concatenation. The Abbey in its centenary year lazily commissioned a brand name and non-playwright. H made a version for middle class Ireland and the Tory Westminister administration both of whom wish to control and hide the Six Counties War. H's version suited the cosy mind-set of the South who 'believe' that North of Sligo, Monaghan, Cavan, and Louth is a landmass where the road signs replicate ancient mapmakers who named undesirable regions with *Hic Sunt Leones* pretending they are unknown territory.

Eileen Battersby in the *Irish Times* (a newspaper mildly left-wing and staunchly conservative: *keep out of my jacuzzi and I will keep out of yours*) was immediately in on the consensus to this 'foundation text of European theatre' (Battersby *Irish Times* 55). No one of sensibility would deny any line of Sophocles in a good translation, but only in the hands of acutely knowledgeable poets who know/knew their Greek. You can only ingest Sophocles or almost, via translations from Dryden, Pope, Browning, Pound, MacNiece, even R. C. Jebb, and such practitioners—these poets loved their Hellenics, and it is the only chance for non-natives to get any flavour of the great Grecian writer. But of course, in comes the

Abbey, stuck for stage material as usual, indeed permanently stuck for stage material, and how to spend their nine million grant.

So, marry off H and Sophocles and it will look great on the publicity and the programmes. A trip back to ancient Greece by none-other than H. Oh wow! However, H confidently stated 'Greek tragedy is as much a musical score as it is a dramatic script' (Hardwick 228). So you can see how he is *not* capable. Battersby quotes H through the usual *Irish Times* narrow sources, 'I read Conor Cruise O'Brien in the *Listener* using *Antigone* to illuminate the conflict in Northern Ireland.' Illuminate! BBC journalism illuminating the North of Ireland under the close eye of the Broadcasting Standards Committee (of British Tories).

My case is easy, Cruise O'Brien guru on the North of Ireland, the *Listener*, Sophocles, and H, therefore for Battersby and *Irish Times*: that's all sorted. If your conscience is really at you, why not get along to the Abbey and see H's *The Burial at Thebes* burying the North of Ireland for the price of a theatre ticket, and if you have a designated-driver, you can get pissed during the interval so the second half of the play goes quicker for you. In point of fact, a plethora of Abbey hangers on, had brought in their own *Antigones*, one by Abbey long term resident Conall Morrison. H is quoted 'my first consideration was speakability' (Battersby) and his version is surely plain speakable. It chatters alright. It is Sophocles done into soap opera. Battersby with a nod to H, has to admit the 'majestic rendition of *Beowulf* caught the essential quasi-pagan, quasi-Christian grandeur of the great Anglo-Saxon epic, and brought it beyond the universities to a wider reading public' (Battersby). Beowulf is not Anglo-Saxon: it is Norse but the *Irish Times* inform the arts culture of the Republic. This is sycophantic sloppy literary journalism. Quasi-journalism.

H props this up and decides to push in the Iraq war as being part of the Sophoclean terrain and sure why not it's a frikken mess of a script already in his paws. 'You are in favour of state security or you are not' (Hardwick 227). Meanwhile his sham-Sophocles plays on a naive politics re-using a phrase as key placename to suggest history adopting the Norman conquered Dublin area known as the Pale. The Chorus uses it and of course Creon 'puts her beyond the pale' (*Thebes* 22). Basically the burial of Polyneices is stretched to make H's point in sophistry within the pretence that this is living theatre engaging with primal and political issues as Ismene reminds her 'In the land of the living, sister' (*Thebes* 5). A much repeated refrain, alas poor H loved his little language snatches so much as to repeat them. He can easily be found screwing up of course where love is 'like a green fern shading/The cheek of a sleeping girl' (*Thebes* 36). Watch H cast Tiresias as half-wit and bring the play toppling down 'my birds in flight/ aren't making any sense' (*Thebes* 44). Or the classic clanger: 'Not if Zeus himself were to send his eagle/To scavenge on that flesh and shit it down' (*Thebes* 44). Yea, yea; no one is a prude anymore perhaps, but come on the metaphor is too awkward, wait until Zeus dumps. Gods are above such, surely.

That Antigone bears no relation to Bush's Iraq war is obvious, and you must place the tragedy amidst a civil war saga to be textually accurate, however the play, as everyone knows except H, is a dynastic drama far better adapted as a patriarchal drama. Creon is the demagogue, a figure not unknown in Ancient Irish Saga. This was Sophocles to Yeats. Creon was both Cuchulain and Conchobar with the *Táin Bó Chuailgne* glossed in for good measure. The Irish household has had many rulers like Chonchobar but H went for his flimsy fake nod to the North of Ireland. The fact that the real actions in the play are blood-bonds inducing suicides is not H territory as I have shown, and how he fled Plath's family saga which she utilised in *Ariel*. H's father-figure is an unrealistic version of his own father, therefore how could he cope with a play that involves family strife that leads to so much death.

Family suicides are often in the news, but H fitted out his version for the Abbey and one could not expect the verse-man to attain any reality. Sophocles was never ruled by sentimentality: the denial of burial to Antigone's brother is state control beyond death. Her suicide and Creon's wife's suicide are the hubris involved but modern audiences don't believe in prophecy, therefore the character of Tiresias could almost be left out. Tiresias re-appears on the modern stage led by Lucky in *Waiting for Godot*. Shakespeare merges him inside Lear. Only real poets believe in prophecy, but H was a shabby verse-man who had a watered down *Irish Times* agnosticism with plenty of RTÉ new-ageism thrown in. H's Tiresias may as well be out of the *Late Late Show* a new-age guru, in fact no more profound that Daniel O'Donnell. When in H's version he says 'birds begin to skirl above my head' (*Thebes* 43) you are in the language of the sheep-faced one who has been flicking through the Anglo-Saxon dictionary again.

Sophocles was constrained by contemporary events and after any Civil War power structures are shaken, the new regime has to stamp out dissidence of all sorts in order to survive but Creon in H's version arguing with Heamon is weak:

You'll rue the day you took it on yourself

To lecture me. You're a real know-nothing (*Thebes* 34).

This is Irish TV drama or haggling in a bus shelter. The corridors of power may possess shards of colloquialism and do, but on stage, centuries of theatre has set a register that a potentate should not talk like an ordinary guy with his girlfriend at a taxi rank on a Saturday night. Or Ismene saying 'My sister is the mainstay of my life' (*Thebes* 26). Yea, obviously but Ismene is fighting the Nazis as it were for her sister's life, and will not deal in lame language, if you are to convey the extremes of the play. H is immune to reality and its rendering, hence his verse.

VI: Heaney's anecdotalism and anecdotage

But to return to the limbo of H's collected poems, and finish the job on hand, as this has been thrust upon me by something of a media furore, having written about H in broadsheet and magazine outlets to outbursts of disapproval for my lengthy reviews. Therefore, here in one book is H and the great poetry hoax.

"Markings" is a boyhood anecdote about youngsters playing ball in a field and a smirch of lines:

There was fleetness, furtherance, untiredness

In time that was extra, unforeseen and free (NSP 88-13; 3).

What's wonky is the utter imprecision—'untiredness' is junior school writing with the inversion of 'time that was extra' that is heavy handed and without the inversion should be 'extra time' as his weary attempt to build in the evocation of so-called endless childhood. "Man and Boy" is a sentimental father-son anecdote with H's inept dialogue—a marked feature of his verse. Had he a pair of ears for anything? H loves the country saws, or sayings but has no talent for finding the richer ones, thus you get a fisherman saying that a salmon was 'As big as a wee pork pig by the sound of it' (NSP 88-13; 5). "Seeing Things" is anecdotalism, and prepare to meet it *ad nauseam* if you are prescribed to read H. This is the weary anecdote of a motor boat journey from Inisboffin, the scene is dashed out in haphazard fashion: 'Sunlight, turfsmoke, seagulls, boatslip, diesel' (NSP 88-13; 7). This is too fast for the ear, eye, or sense to feel any connection with it, as he later grapples after effects such as 'The deep, still, seeable-down-into water' (NSP 88-13; 7). This is embarrassing. H's fear of water is a constant and much alluded to everywhere, yet he never refined this into anything valid in writing: 'seeable-down-into' is weak language usage.

"An August Night" is a three-liner about hands compared to 'two ferrets': 'Playing all by themselves in a moonlit field' (NSP 88-13; 10). This is of course absurd, and makes no connection. The comparison and the moonlight are unaccountably separate. "Field of Vision" shows H in his anecdotage suffering from anecdotalism, when an old woman finds more in the view beyond her window than watching TV. What is implausible is for H to expect any rational person to believe that the old woman who is meant to have for years looked 'Straight out past the TV in the corner' (NSP 88-13; 11) and never watched any TV: this is plainly untrue. More true of the TV era are rural folk watching more TV than landscape, farmyard, or sky, as one supposes they did pre-TV. H's title "Field of Vision" is weak, an obvious lazy word choice but he had to feed Faber their menu as they had prescribed what he should produce.

"The Pitchfork" is hyperbole, and a forced attempt to render heroic a useful implement. H simple does not have the skill to turn his own hay and dross into verse-gold. The melodrama that he invokes about the pitchfork is arch and annoying: 'The springiness, the clip and dart of it' (NSP 88-13; 12): this is laboured excitement, fakery, especially as it neglects the practicality and hard work involved in utilising such tools. H possesses no ability to address the sublime of this potential subject: all is novelty for him, whereas to the pitchfork-user it is a tool. To H, it is like a toy, something you pick up and play with, therefore his verse leads the reader to know that he knows nothing of actual field work, or pitchfork work.

H cannot envisage the potential of such an item as being deadly, this he barely touches on: 'It felt like a javelin, accurate and light' (NSP 88-13; 12) which is immediately repressed, showing that in H there is a complete lack of sensibility, sensitivity, and sharpness of language in the conveyance of reality and emotion. Yes, a pitchfork could be redolent of much perhaps, if used artfully but not in H's handling within verse. H makes a novelty of the farm and farmyard continually. It is a model farm of miniatures, as I stated in VILLAGE, he writes snippets that might suit exhibition notices for an agricultural museum, except his lack of evocation, accuracy, and reality of farm life is not up to standard. He is a fake farmyard-boy, looking back to childhood; using and re-using the same subject matter that becomes jaded for accomplished verse. There is farmyard verse, albeit Robert Frost with his fences and woodpiles and notoriously the "Out, Out—" where a chainsaw causes a death, however, it unfortunately ends with unprepossessing lines ruining his performance:

And they, since they

Were not the one dead, turned to their affairs. (Frost ls. 33-4;136).

My conviction is that if you meet someone wielding a *Collected H* and a *Collected Frost*, you must register their knowledge of poetry is close to zero. Frost is the American H, just as H is the Irish Frost, but in fairness Frost is way ahead in achievement.

"The Settle Bed" (back to H!) is a version of the *auld song* "Grandma's Feather Bed" especially 'Imagine a dower of settle beds tumbled from heaven' (NSP 88-13; 13) it fails as surrealism because the topic is nostalgia. What is a dower of settle beds? No one knows. "Glanmore Revisted" is a sonnet sequence for example: "Scrabble"

Year after year, our game of Scrabble: love

Taken for granted like any other word (NSP 88-13; 15)

a genuine poetry reader cannot accept this obviousness. "The Cot" gapes towards its conclusion that is prompted in earlier lines:

the same cot I myself slept in

When the whole world was a farm that eked and crowed (NSP 88-13; 16).

"A Pillowed Head" is so awful, it beggars description, while "Wheels within Wheels" is obviously about learning to cycle a bicycle, and H turning a bicycle upside down to turn the peddles 'like a mill-wheel pouring at the treadles' (NSP 88-13; 24). H's metaphors are always melodramatic, and in terms of poetical value: nil because their exaggerative parameters distract from any connection with the subject. H in collection after collection repeats himself, hence the vague establishment of his subject matter. The repetition is, of course, a glaring proof of limitations. A real poet could fit out the page length of H's verse, but H, devoid of inspiration, had soon used up his oblique unrealised farmyard themes. Suddenly, instead of the nostalgic drama of learning to ride a bike, the verse becomes obsessed with the world of the mill. A wheel suggests a millwheel as he abandons the bicycle-content of the verse. Does he mean a unicycle? One does not know.

"Fosterling" is *faux* nostalgic, unbelievably inaccurate, and of course melodramatic:

Me waiting until I was nearly fifty

To credit marvels (NSP 88-13; 25).

"Lightenings" and "Settings" pursue their own sporadic memories as in 'xv' when he recalls his father (yet again) getting a lamp to fetch the 'the unbleeding, vivid-flesh bacon' out of a tea chest (NSP 88-13; 38). Of course, it's 'unbleeding' (crass usage in H's un-verse non-verse). This 'event' leads to: 'That night I owned the piled grain of Egypt' (NSP 88-13; 38).

It is hyperbole verging on hysteria. The sequences are meant to be visionary, incidentally, so he puts in at random, in brackets as the last line of xxii: "(Set questions for the ghost of W.B.)" (NSP 88-13; 40). One comes across anachronisms continually, when describing water as 'laden' thus: 'Laden high Atlantic' (NSP 88-13; 41). "Crossings" follows similar evocations as in "Lightenings".

His father is quoted in xxvii and is pitched at the heights of sentimentality giving advice to a young woman going to London:

Look for a man with an ashplant on the boat,

[...] and stay near him all night//

And you'll be safe. (NSP 88-13; 42).

This is provincial, it may be an accurate recounting, but it shows an innocence that is not realistic of the region; as if any woman would at random stay beside a farmer and 'be safe' just because he is a cattle drover with an ashplant. The logic of folklore lacks realism since folklore is not about absolute innocence. The H-anecdotes make nonsense of folklore and reality.

H can be said to be quaintly-encyclopaedic, and focuses in the opening lines on a door latch in "Crossings" no. (xxix):

Scissors-and-slap abruptness of a latch.

Its coldness to the thumb. Its see-saw lift

And drop and innocent harshness. (NSP 88-13; 43)

This does not need to be versified, it is utterly banal and useless. H's limited writing is about what is actually not universal rural experience but in stating banalities as in xxxii: 'Running water never disappointed' (NSP 88-13; 45) and 'Stepping stones were stations of the soul' (NSP 88-13; 45). All this is false profundity but the reader is assured that 'It steadies me to tell these things' (NSP 88-13; 45). What gauche self-consciousness.

"Squarings" is about the basalt Giant's Causeway, the wellknown North of Ireland wonder of archaeology, where a throne of rock is pushed into the folklore, a place for H to make a wish. He turns the verse into tourist material, as the speaker describes 'The small of your back made very solid sense' (NSP 88-13; 51). It is a tourist caption and a poor one. The revelation at this vantage point of seascape and landscape is: 'But you were only goose-fleshed skin and bone' (NSP 88-13; 51). A few sonnets further more profundity—?—'Was music once a proof of God's existence? (NSP 88-13; 58). "Crossings" is difficult to get through because of its attempts at philosophy that are excessively dull.

"Mint" makes one ask: surely H knew the difference between nettles and mint which he describes in the opening lines:

It looked like a clump of small dusty nettles

Growing wild at the gable of the house (NSP 88-13; 62).

After a while, ploughing through H's stuff, there is the relief of laughter at the ludicrous 'Let the smells of mint go heady and defenceless' (NSP 88-13; 62) this is funny. H is so serious, so utterly, serious.

Meanwhile (yawn, yawn) "A Sofa in the Forties" is a rehash of "The Settle-Bed": 'Its castors on tiptoe' (NSP 88-13; 63); again Granny's Feather Bed is taken out to play; this time it's an auld sofa. "Keeping Going" is for his brother Hugh, and a recollection full of anecdotes: the white wash brush, the tractor into Derry, milking the cows; why he has to drag in a scene from Lady Macbeth and comment 'I felt at home with that one all right' (NSP 88-13; 67).

"Two Lorries" is anecdotal and descriptive, pushing metaphors and the weak comedy about "Young Agnew" the coalman becoming a fantasy of his mother's referred to in the closing lines with a previous assertion 'sweet-talk darkness, coalman' (NSP 88-13; 70) 'Dreamboat coalman filmed in silk-white ashes' (NSP 88-13; 70). These conclusions are pushed into the usual H-fake as he ludicrously sees death as the coalman (it's zany and crazy):

Death walked out past her like a dust-faced coalman

Refolding body-bags, plying his load

Empty upon empty, in a flurry (NSP 88-13; 70)

Basically trying to poeticise a delivery of coal as death is stagey forced pantomime. And what sort of corpse would fit into a sack of coal? It is so hopelessly vague, hit and miss, and inappropriate.

"St Kevin and the Blackbird" takes an existing legend of miraculous event from the Irish Saint's Life, but it did not happen in Glendalough, and what H spoils in melodrama is the saint praying and who dares not move his hands because a bird is building a nest within them. The saga, myth, and miracle is about Kevin (Coemgen) aged 7 in Cornwall praying during the Lenten period in patience, piety and love of God's creatures, and a mother bird hatching out her fledglings.

Unfortunately, H is not able to echo the myth but instead uses it sentimentally, and as you would expect, in stating the obvious about saintliness in transcendence with Kevin 'on the riverbank forgotten the river's name' (NSP 88-13; 77) in the act of meditation and prayer. This highlights the limits of H's expression: obvious, trite and shallow.

Just as "Damson" re-uses the idea of the bricklayer as heroic 'I loved especially the trowel's shine' (SL 15). Trowels are used by builders and others. The shine is soon gone, but for H it is apparently only a trowel when it is shiny and new.

Trowel wielder, woundie, drive them off

Like Odysseus in Hades lashing out (SL 16).

"Flight Path" Section 4 (a rare event for H) is mention of the North of Ireland Sectarian War (1968-1998) when Ciaran Nugent is a prisoner of the Thatcher British regime, and where H has to assume Dantescan proportions in mentioning and claiming the following:

Like something out of Dante's scurfy hell,

Drilling their way through the rhymes and images

Where I too walked behind the righteous Virgil

As safe as houses and translating freely (NSP 88-13; 79)

Claiming to walk behind Virgil is absurd. The problem here, in fact, the infamy here is not the super Faber & Faber ego but the inaccuracies. Revolutionaries like Ciaran Nugent, jailed and claiming political status does not enter the poem, and this requires to be glossed outside the lines. In terms of 'poetry' the adjectives 'scurfy' and 'righteous' do not fit, would never fit: it is impossible to summon up Dante's hell, and Virgil as a person and poet in a single adjective and only one, such as H uses, which was part of the ego-fostered imago that fed the so-called 'poems'. When Nugent appears as a member of the IRA (actually Danny Morrison) and asks H:

'When, for fuck's sake, are you going to write

Something for us?' 'If I do write something,

Whatever it is, I'll be writing for myself.' (NSP 88-13; 79)

There is H's position, and it is furthermore compounded by his admission of not attending the funeral of Francis Hughes (1956-1981), a neighbour in County Derry, and the second person to die on Hunger Strike for political status in The Maze prison. H's comment on avoiding Hughes's funeral was 'I would have been wary of the political implication of attendance' (RP, 187). Of Hughes, he noted, 'his parents and elder sisters were well known to me' (StepSton, 222). He is also trenchant about which side he is on: 'If I had been at home in Dublin, I still would not have travelled the hundred miles north to the wake' (RP, 187). The Hunger Strikers followed 'the fatal logic of their choice' (RP, 187). H's stance is pro-Thatcher because in his own words to attend the funeral 'would have been an endorsement of the violent means and programmes of the Provisional IRA' (RP, 187). H's national identity is in this: 'I grew up in the minority in Northern Ireland and was educated within the dominant British culture' (RP, 202). That proves it: he is British, a nationalist turned Loyalist because of allegiance to Faber & Faber. This is a shameful, cowardly admission for one of his background.

H was in Oxford University as guest of Charles Monteith that day and noted of Hughes, 'he was also a hit man and his Protestant neighbours would have considered him involved in something like a war of genocide against them rather than a war of liberation against occupying forces of the crown. At that stage the IRA's self-image as liberators didn't work much magic with me. But neither did the too-brutal simplicity of Margaret Thatcher's "A crime is a crime is a crime. It is not political"' (StepStone, 260). Unfortunately, as James Connolly stated there is no such as thing as a glorious war but you are one side or another: there is no neutrality in a sectarian war.

H did visit the wake of Thomas McElwee, another of the hunger strikers: 'It gave some relief to me, at least. The family would have known that I wasn't an IRA supporter, but they would have also known that this crossing of their threshold was above and beyond the politics that were distracting everybody' (StepStone 260). 'Politics that were distracting everybody'—this is middleclass repressive avoidance of the unfinished business of the Irish Question. This mention of 'politics' is rhetoric and bluff on H's part. Two fingers to the North, and the struggle that began in Nationalist North of Ireland in 1968 for equality, human rights, and a United Ireland. H states clearly that he can be counted out. Such is his definitive politics which is pro-British.

Similarly a cohort of H's, Michael Longley cashed in on 'the Troubles' as Arts Council Director, when the *Irish Times* published a 'poem' by Longley entitled "Ceasefire" where he presumes to 'borrow' the Homeric grandeur of the *Iliad* with rank ineptitude in trying to equalise the Loyalist and Nationalist positions in the imperialist-bound and trapped Six Counties. Longley's use of Hector bearing Achilles's corpse is so far removed from the North's unresolved situation, as to be a disgusting and cheapening of its seriousness in the fake presentation of Unity between historically and violently opposed sides as Plantation people versus dispossessed Irish Nationalists together on Irish soil. The real history of the Irish Six Counties is not fiction or fake. But Longley, obviously, knew that the Trojan War was not a land war and went ahead pushing himself into pseudo-Homeric proportions for a gullible poetry readership of academics and others, indicative of cosy comments, such as 'the canonical poetry of Homer is thus integrated with contemporary events, the authority of the Greek text providing a parallel to the Northern Ireland's memorable recent history' (Robson 232). Memorable! It is incredibly insulting and undignified, to place such a statement upon the slaughtered dead Nationalists that theirs was a 'memorable recent history'.

"Mycenae Lookout" shows H unwieldy as in the line 'Where the blaze would leap the hills when Troy had fallen' (NSP 88-13; 80):

The agony of Clytemnestra's love-shout

That rose through the palace like the yell of troops

Hurled by King Agamemnon from the ships. (NSP 88-13; 81).

What is 'wrong' here is that Clytemnestra's shout is from her alone, and is forced and confused by referring to the 'troops', but H is stuck again and requires melodrama to buttress up his lack of facility with language, imagination, and poetry. H has to 'turn' the ancient Greek history towards the farmyard, such is the lack of perspective:

in the bountiful round mouths of iron pumps

and gushing taps. (NSP 88-13; 89).

The problem is that the discordant pump and taps refer to H's 1940s but there were no taps in ancient Greece; he means that his childhood is so redolent and present to him that Greek civilisation reminds him of his beloved taps, and of course that ineffably dull farmyard. H breeds a hatred of his locale which is surely not the prescript of his verse as he wants the reader to love his native turf and farm.

"The Gravel Walks" takes the reader back to H's familiar farm, field, and this time a bit of building to break the monotony because nothing happens on the farm in H-land.

And cement mixers began to come to life

And men in dungarees, like captive shades (NSP 88-13; 90).

Again melodrama in 'captive shades'. Gravel is forced into various metaphorical places such as 'The Pharaoh's brickyards burned inside their heads' (NSP 88-13; 90). H is forced into pushing it all too far, in saying 'The kingdom of gravel was inside you too -' (NSP 88-13; 91). He means that for H, the verse-maker, every human activity is eventually seen as the equivalent to making verse: it is so inhuman and antipathetic and light years away from poetry.

In a "Poet's Chair" he heads straight for the metaphor and Socrates is soon on board in Athens facing execution. It simply doesn't work. When you read the following BS:

I am all foreknowledge.

Of the poem as a ploughshare that turns time

Up and over. (NSP 88-13; 94)

'Foreknowledge' is such a bungled term as to be utterly useless. It fails totally. And, it holds the usual claims for verse-making because he is ultimately the verse-man. Yes, he's swamped with nostalgia but it is very unpalatable as in "The Swing" which reads like the *For Dummies Series* 'Teach Yourself How To Swing':

To start up by yourself, you hitched the rope

Against your backside and backed on into it (NSP 88-13; 96).

Again he reaches the melodramatic and the ludicrous in cross-referencing Hiroshima which is woefully out of place:

We all learned one by one to go sky high.

Then townlands vanished into aerodromes,

Hiroshima made light of human bones (NSP 88-13; 96).

"Two Stick Drawings" is about a local woman who could knock down a blackberry from a high briar with a stick, and which takes him a page and a half to tell, except that

Persephone

Was in the halfpenny place compared to Claire. (NSP 88-13; 97).

The use of Persephone has no place or justification. "At the Wellhead" is about a blindwoman but all these people from his childhood, whatever their circumstances and existence, cannot grab much attention. They are remote as faded photographs. It is like hearing someone talk of their relatives and neighbours whom one has never met or known, there is no union of commonality or universality to make it engaging. H simply cannot achieve anything much in verse. "At Banagher" continues the sepia snapshot portrayals with an anecdote about a tailor who is chorused to high heaven and exalted thus:

My Lord Buddha of Banagher, the way

Is opener for your being in it (NSP 88-13; 109).

The image of Buddha is never that of a tailor. Besides, the Buddha is never dressed the way a North of Ireland tailor would dress. But for H the tailor kinda sits like a Buddha at his work. Did you never think of that, well H did. Isn't he terrific with words and images, just ask Charlie What's His Teeth. 'Opener' is really the wrong word too, of course, one gets it (ho-hum) and the tailor is worthy of praise but not in this sentimental tone. Verse such as this is no more than weak verse and pretty poor stuff as folklore claiming to be poetry. H uses the word 'garment' accurate of the time, but "Postscript" is revealing of his usual deficiencies. Verse is stretched to make a moment of assumed importance when he parks his car on a windy day 'As big soft buffetings come at the car sideways' (NSP 88-13; 111). Obviously, it was a windy day and this happens to parked cars: wouldn't you weep for the poor vehicles perishing there in the cold. Was H an imbecile? No, he was just mass producing low quality verse for Faber & Faber to maintain his career.

"Perch": 'Perch we called "grunts"' (NSP 88-13; 120) and this permits him to wallow in dialect but the verse is a mere description of the river fish 'on carpets of Bann stream' because the river could sort-of look like a carpet (NSP 88-13; 120). "Lupins" is given similar treatment:

That stood their ground for all our summer wending

[...]And even when they blanched would never balk (NSP 88-13; 121).

The usual imprecision and melodrama, and the Hopkins' hangover with the heavy assonance. However, lupins do not stand their ground like humans, nor do flowers blush or balk. It's all twee, and more suitable for verse for children, perhaps. "Out of the Bag" has his stock in trade colloquialism: family folklore commentary, 'All of us came in Dr Kerlin's bag.' (NSP 88-13; 122). So, here we go down the sentimental trail to the birth of the H-clan. Dr Kerlin, of course, needs a metaphor carrying his bag and this is a whopper of a metaphor:

'With the bag in his hand, a plump ark by the keel...' (NSP 88-13; 122).

Kerlin is carrying Noah's ark by the keel, get it? Yea, amazing. Can the closing lines about the mother be justified in any verse form; could they *ever be* in a real poem? Of course they may have been uttered, but they are utterly banal and trite, and more suitable to anecdotal reminiscence than pulling their weight in three so-called lines of 'poetry':

And what do you think

Of the new wee baby the doctor brought for us all

When I was asleep? (NSP 88-13; 124).

The syntax is lamentable and deplorable. Furthermore, especially on a farm and in rural life, children are not simpletons and know where 'babies' come from since they've seen rural farmyard life, death and birth. The doctor does not 'bring' a baby, no more than the Vet brings a 'calf' or a 'foal'. In fact, as anecdote, H does not achieve the status or richness of real anecdote.

In "The Little Canticles of Asturias" apparently in the 'valley of Gijon' he is transported back to 'the house-thatch' (NSP 88-13; 125) rather than Compostela. He is unable to be there in Compostela, such is the call out, or call back to Mossbawn and Bellaghy, his native turf calling him once more which was his shallow neurotic infantilism. "Ballynahinch Lake" and

A pair of waterbirds splashed up and down

And on and on (NSP 88-13; 127)

'pair' is awkward, and 'on and on' woefully bad. The big moment is the starting of a car engine, and being distracted by 'air-heavers, far heavier than the air' (NSP 88-13; 127). Basically, the birds out on the lake are being called air-heavers. Yes, it's an absolutely frightening mis-use of language, and of course there is a sort of sham New Ageism about birds and car pollution. Basically, he would try anything; but cannot kick start the sloppy mess into a poem.

"The Clothes Shrine" is where 'Light white muslin blouses' are drying on the line which evokes

St Brigid once more

Had rigged up a ray of sun

[...]To dry her own cloak on (NSP 88-13; 128).

Yea, that's it; that's all you get of St Brigid, however H gets it wrong. Brigid is patron of the wool trade and thus a piece of lamb's wool, reputedly from the Irish saint's garment is preserved in a reliquary in Bruges. "Glanmore Eclogue" is a dismal dialogue between Myles and Poet. Myles says that Poet has no 'blisters on your hand nor weather-worries.'(NSP 88-13; 130) and asks for a song which Poet duly complies with about birds. There is a whopper-metaphor: 'Bog-cotton bows to moorland wind' and 'Bogbanks shine like ravens' wings.' (NSP 88-13; 131). Very awkward and impossible connections. "Sonnets for Hellas" contrast memories of Mossbawn with Greece when a lorry load of apples

had burst open on the road[...]

our tyres raunched and scrunched them

But we drove on [...] (NSP 88-13; 132).

"Conkers" is about 'looted conkers/Gravid in my satchel, swinging nicely'. (NSP 88-13; 133) There is no need for the gravid or looted. He means stolen apples.

"Pylos" mentions his Harvard colleague, Professor Robert Fitzgerald but H is triumphantly feeling like Telemachus for some reason: 'Young again in the whitewashed light of morning' (NSP 88-13; 134). "The Augean Stables" continues the sham-Homeric parallel, and likens a murdered Catholic, Sean Brown, a GAA player from Bellaghy (but the awful clanger closing line): 'In the car park where his athlete's blood ran cold' (NSP 88-13; 135). The pun is inappropriate. The insensitive use of language is offensive.

"Vitruviana" claims exceptionalism as H wades into a pool of water:

Up to the chest, then stood there half-suspended

Like Vitruvian man, both legs wide apart,

Both arms out buoyant to the fingertips (NSP 88-13; 138).

He remembers ball games at boarding school but is living in Dublin 4—the city's affluent quarter, far from farmyards. "Audenesque" *in memory of Joseph Brodsky* is H in rhyming quatrains (aa/bb) imitating Auden's elegy for Yeats which becomes more exercise than heartfelt plaint, and the rhymes are often halved:

Pepper vodka you produced

Once in Western Massachusetts (NSP 88-13; 140).

There can be no claims in the elegy to face Brodsky's complex politics and history as in '(West that meant for you, of course,/Lenin's train-trip in reverse.)' (NSP 88-13; 140).

"Anahorish 1944" is a remembrance of the US Troops in the North of Ireland (with nothing original from H): 'they tossed us gum and tubes of coloured sweets.' (NSP 88-13; 147). Actually reads like from sources rather than actual experience (NSP 88-13; 147).

"Anything Can Happen" is from Horace Odes i., 34 reflecting the Twin Towers destruction and loss of life in NY. Significantly, there is no comment, no reportage as to the global conflict, merely 'nothing resettles right' (NSP 88-13; 148). It is a political non-sequitur at a time of upheaval. Basically, he had nothing to say. None of it moved him to utter.

"District and Circle" grasps after a happy time in life with its underground imagery but the collection of this name soon repeats and repeats the old reliable farm stuff, as in "The Turnip Snedder": 'This is the way God sees life,' it said, 'from seedling braird to snedder' (D&C 3). Can H know how God sees life? This is how H sees life.

"The Harrow-Pin":

We'd be told, "If you don't behave

There'll be nothing in your Christmas stocking for you

But an old kale stalk." And we would believe him. (D&C, 23).

In Ireland 'stocking' refers to nylons worn by females. 'Christmas Stocking' is an Americanism; whereas local to H's countryside, people hung their sock up at Christmas not their stocking.

"The Birch Grove" concludes that if art teaches nothing 'it's that the human condition is private' (D&C, 72). This is H's innate prudery. Well, now you know, you've heard it from the aficionado farmyard, pump, kitchen-sink verse-maker.

"Stern" is dedicated to Ted Hughes about Eliot, King of Faber but the metaphor, obviously Hughes's is one of those gargantuan ones, comparing the American poet of *The Waste Land* to 'the prow of the *Queen Mary*' (NSP 88-13; 162). The comparison is simply not there while the point of homage is made, or just about, but the comparison is relative and not anything 'poetic'. Eliot as 'stern' based on the pun within his full name 'Thomas Stearns Eliot' and comparing the American poet to a liner are woefully awkward.

"Out of This World" to Czeslaw Milosz is not an elegy, more a recollection of communion in church, and how it relates to the

undying

tremor and draw, like well water far below (NSP 88-13; 163).

Whatever about H and matters of religious belief, I would contest
that the introduction of, even the comparison with well-water is
more of his usual stock in trade. In fact, H had used up his so called
beloved farm, field, and environs, very early on in his versifying and
as it turns out in the later pieces, it is really threadbare and hollow:
so much turf mould, out of which no fire could be made. From some
ashes, no phoenix shall ever rise: this is H's situation.

"In Iowa" among the Mennonites, he finds a mowing machine

where wilted corn stalks flagged the snow,

A mowing machine (NSP 88-13; 164).

It's pathetic: as he swanned about Iowa but cheesily he can only
come up with a grinning piece of farm machinery. Is this meant to be
orgasmic about a mowing machine? Hardly, but in hyperbole he tries
it out. He goes for it, and as usual flops beginning with a Biblical
word:

Verily I came forth from that wilderness

As one unbaptized who had known darkness

At the third hour and the veil in tatters. (NSP 88-13; 164).

Isn't this a vainglorious lout of a pose in verse? It becomes cloying as in "The Tollund Man in Springtime":

I was like turned turf in the breath of God,

Bog-bodied on the sixth day, brown and bare (NSP 88-13; 166).

It is High Infants Bible Class talk from a grown man. The Tollund man is now feeling modernity: 'Heard from my heather bed the thickened traffic' (NSP 88-13; 167). 'And transatlantic flights stacked in the blue' (NSP 88-13; 167). It is a persona poem, remotely placed from past to present without any effect, except the obvious premeditated structure. A kind of, imagine you are a Tollund man from prehistory and living in the present, what would you see. Now write a few lines, put in traffic and aeroplanes. He forgot to mention laptops and mobile phones. It is all useless speculation, as to what a Tollund man would think of modernity. "Planting the Alder" is a piece of Hopkinesque pastiche at this late stage of his career. "Quitting Time" is back in the farmyard hosing it down: you've guessed it: 'the cast-iron pump immobile as a herm', yes *herm* (NSP 88-13; 172) they usually are and he throws in: 'The song of a tubular steel gate in the dark' (NSP 88-13; 172).

"Had I not been awake" is worse:

A wind that rose and whirled until the roof

Pattered with quick leaves off the sycamore//

And got me up, the whole of me a-patter,

Alive and ticking like an electric fence. (NSP 88-13; 175)

What a woeful anecdote that no-one would listen to; this is sham-emotion recollected in senility. What was he wired to at all? Ticking? And like an electric fence. Ask the farmers; an electric fence only ticks when it is short circuited; normally, it has a low hum when the current is working properly. A case of H's robotic verse causing a malfunction on the electric fence.

"Album" as you'd imagine has nostalgia about the fact that he had hardly ever embraced his father; and all in five sections. "The Conway Stewart" is about the fountain pen and filling it with ink which is compared to:

its first deep snorkel

In a newly opened ink-bottle (NSP 88-13; 181)

and the sounds it makes, ingesting ink are 'Guttery, snottery,' (NSP 88-13; 181).

"Chanson d'Aventure" cannot avoid nostalgia, as he recalls ringing the bells in chapel in school. "Human Chain" is back in the farmyard, and with a dedication to one of his fans, Professor Terence Browne of TCD, as many of H's verses repay favourable critiques over the years with debts settled. 'Seeing the bags of meal passed hand to hand' (NSP 88-13; 190). "The Baler" and a local man named as Derek Hill saying:

He could bear no longer to watch

The Sun going down

And asking please to be put

With his back to the window. (NSP 88-13; 191-192).

There is nothing erotic in H, except by insertion of an anecdote from Walter de la Mare about seeing a tree struck by lightning in "Eelworks": 'The bark came off it//Like a girl taking off her petticoat' (NSP 88-13; 195). Yes, one does not see or feel anything feminine in H's stilted words.

"Route 110" is a recollection of Belfast and being homeward bound on the Cookstown bus, and various other recalls, very uninteresting with the local mish-mash of random memories. "The door was open and the house was dark" is a poem title taken from fellow scribe, David Hammond and in memoriam. H-clumsiness prevails as it clunks to a vapid conclusion:

Emptiness, as in a midnight hangar//

On an overgrown airfield in late summer (NSP 88-13; 214)

There is a slight reference to the Bloody Sunday massacre in Derry. "In the Attic" reflects old age, dreaming of being like Robert Louis Stevenson's Jim Hawkins.

"A Mite-Box" from *The Human Chain* sticks to his old material: this time 'an alms-collecting mite-box' as a child going door to door collecting and the conclusion 'A way for all to see a way to heaven' (HC 19). The box is compared to a *camera obscura* at the close of the piece. Well, he has to stretch out the lines, and fill at least some parts of the page for Faber, or there would be a blank book. For as it is, most of them barely fill out the centre of the pages. H's little versicles, you know.

"Slack":

The sound it made

More to me

Than any allegory (HC 33).

And:

Tipped and slushed

Catharsis

From the bag. (HC 34).

Yes, this must be how he felt about slack, that form of watered down coal, hence you have the pity-seeking image but finally that this fuel provided catharsis? Does anyone in God's creation who is human, understand how the evocation of slack could provide the Aristotelian feature of catharsis? H's verse generally presents fake feelings, whereas poetry can convey various states of intense emotion amidst other poetical attributes, and certainly fails when the resonance is pretence to what is clearly not felt in the lines. A bag of catharsis does not catch fire in this case, in H's "Slack". The title is reflexively accurate: it is slack verse. I have done with this business except for the 'Afterword: Heaney's toxic cult' which concludes the book.

Heaney: poet of farmyard, bogs and prehistory

The published version in *Village: a magazine of politics and culture* was edited from the following Draft:

Kevin Kiely

Seamus Heaney's qualities as Irish cultural minister without portfolio, his teaching in Harvard and Oxford, the long list of awards including a Nobel Prize as well as endorsements of institutions, publications and arts all stemmed from his profile as a poet. He, of course, avoided addressing the sectarian conflict in the North of Ireland and instead utilised mythology and archaeology but found his real subject down on the farm, close by the sights and sounds of the bog. This preoccupation with bogs increased as he wrote about bog corpses, skeletons and bones which safely distanced him from the war. Meanwhile, his admirers explained that he was actually obliquely engaging with the North. However, Heaney's most trenchant utterance in 2013 was surprisingly non-Nationalist for someone of his background: "There's never going to be a united Ireland. So why don't you let them [Loyalists] fly the flag?" Heaney's squeaky clean content was always non-political up to this utterance. Bill Clinton on his visit to Derry in March used Heaney's phrase from Sophocles in translation that occasionally 'hope and history rhyme'. Such jingles are dangerously trite when making speeches about the Six Counties. Basically, Heaney is a poet of nostalgia for home and hearth, the turf-fire, the hen house and the bicycle. His accessibility to readers equalled Maeve Binchy whose chick-lit is slightly more modern in content.

Meanwhile, many academics and passive Eng. Lit. students felt secure reading Heaney because of his London publisher, Faber & Faber. Among academic critics who lavished praise on him, were Harold Bloom and Helen Vendler both of Harvard with John Carey of Oxford, and others such as Blake Morrison and Neil Corcoran.

All of these were comfortable in following the American poet Robert Lowell's misguided high-praise that Heaney was 'the best Irish poet since Yeats'. Lowell's backer was T. S. Eliot, justly acknowledged as *the* supreme modernist poet and founding-director of Faber & Faber. After Eliot's demise, Charles Monteith from Lisburn, took over and reflected a taste in poetry from his milieu as former London barrister. Monteith was a friend of Louis MacNeice, also a Faberman with W. H. Auden, Lowell, John Berryman and Ted Hughes. Hughes brought to Faber, albeit posthumously, the poetry of his legendary ex-wife, Sylvia Plath. Monteith's mission in the 1960s aimed to maintain Faber's illustrious legacy in poetry. Firstly, through Richard Murphy, a fellow Oxonian of Monteith's and finally, Heaney who would later haul into Faber one of his students at QUB, namely, Paul Muldoon.

Monteith's 'finding' Heaney in the 1960s at the beginning of the war proved to be good for business. Heaney had the pejorative Northman caché and was decidedly a 'safe' poet. Monteith rushed out four collections in a decade followed by Heaney's *Selected Poems*. There was the added bonus of media coverage when Heaney went into permanent exile in Dublin in 1972 with a summer house in Wicklow while being flown about in the Faber helicopter on poetry reading tours. Heaney's wife Marie Heaney née Devlin, coincidentally brother of Barry Devlin of *Horslips* ensured the poet's easy entrée to RTÉ's arts programming. Heaney stuck by his farmyard themes and continually ploughed the same furrow even in later collections with their mawkish titles: *Field Work, The Haw Lantern* and *Opened Ground*. Under Professor John L. Sweeney's recommendation, Harvard reeled him in and Oxford soon followed by offering the Professor of Poetry position. The Nobel Laureateship sealed the issue with an assured brand name in poetry: *Famous* Seamus Heaney.

Heaney's poetry in terms of literature, rarely if ever, leaves the farmstead for its subject matter. When you read a poem entitled "Thatcher" it is not about politics and certainly not about Maggie the British PM. All of his pastoral work is nostalgic and anecdotal with titles such as "Churning Day" ; "The Forge" ; "Gifts of Rain" ; "Blackberry-Picking" ; "Turkeys Observed" ; "The Harrow-Pin" ; "Conkers" ; "The Seed Cutters" ; "Nostalgia in the Afternoon" ; "A Basket of Chestnuts" ; "The Pitchfork" ; "The Settle Bed" ; "The Sandpit" ; "Bog Oak" ; "The Hill Farm" ; "The Water Carrier" ; "At A Potato Digging" ; "The Gravel Walks" ; "The Skylight" ; "The Baler" ; "Fireside" and "At the Wellhead". Heaney's obsession with the farm is about as redolent as a visit to an agricultural folklore museum where you can buy a toy farmyard for the kids in the souvenir shop.

To criticise Heaney's poetry in the Irish media is not permitted, and to do so in company is usually disapproved and viewed as being untutored in official verse culture. Mainstream reviewers as well as academic journals never dare to speak out against his work except for two analytical essays: Desmond Fennell's "Whatever You Say, Say Nothing" (1991) and James Simmons's in "The Trouble with Seamus" (1992). When Eamon Dunphy criticised Heaney as 'a sham national poet' in 1995 in *The Sunday Independent* he was seen as attacking a sacred cow. Dunphy's commentary is valid when one reads Heaney's poem in praise of bovine pregnancy titled "Cow in calf". However, there is a Heaney mafia mainly academic that endeavour to maintain their guru poet as an untouchable literary demagogue. Despite his image as cultural icon he was a Nobel poet who never equalled the achievements in literature of Shaw, Yeats, Joyce and Beckett. Heaney's Nobel acceptance speech lacked vigour: 'I credit poetry, in other words, both for being itself and for being a help...I credit it because credit is due to it, in our time and in all time, for its truth to life, in every sense of that phrase.' This clearly reveals Heaney's own depth of insight with regard to poetry in using weak sentiments while analysing the art form as nothing more than being itself, and always deserving credit basically because of its truth-to-life factor! Hardly a major revelation but everything to do with his work is definitely not major when you read him in full.

Heaney's lack of engagement with the Northern conflict was clearly evidenced early on in "Summer 1969". 'While the Constabulary covered the mob/Firing into the Falls, I was suffering/Only the bullying sun of Madrid.' The poem concludes with his retreating for the 'cool of the Prado' to look at Goya's painting 'Shootings of the Third of May'. This sort of cultural tourism and pretence to sympathy for the North while on holiday, cooling off in exotic cities and protecting your own hide was fairly typical of his deliberately lazy political content.

Heaney's best-known poem "Digging" ludicrously compares a pen to a gun to a shovel! It begins: 'Between my finger and my thumb/The squat pen rests; snug as a gun'. It's inaccurate, of course, in that a gun is not usually held between finger and thumb like a pen: a hand-gun has to be held using all fingers. Heaney makes claims in the poem that his grandfather could cut more turf in a day 'than any other man'. This reflects his standard trademark: anecdotes chopped into lines of verse. Finally in "Digging", he views himself as unfit for farm work or turf cutting having only his pen, and concludes: 'I'll dig with it.' In the introduction to his translation of *Beowulf* he admitted his passion for 'a nostalgia I didn't know I suffered until I experienced its fulfillment'. This fulfillment of nostalgia saturates his final collection *The Human Chain* typically set in the old familiar farmyard. The title poem is about lifting grain onto a trailer 'with a grip on two sack corners'.

Posterity is the ultimate judge. Popular reputations fade. Poetry oblivion is a huge institution haunted by once over-rated literary reputations including William Allingham, Padraic Colum, James Stephens, and among British poet laureates, Robert Southey, Alfred

Austin, John Masefield and Cecil Day-Lewis. Thomas Moore and Robert Burns are latterly rated not as poets but as mere song-writers. Heaney had no songs. He is not very quotable at all as witnessed in the obituaries that rehashed the most predictable lines from his poem "Digging". The poem is, of course illogical, if not silly since no-one ever digs with a pen, and to suggest such to a farmer in a farming environment would lead to utter ridicule. Heaney's metaphor of comparing writing to digging ultimately falls flat, since in any event, he didn't get much deeper than the top soil.

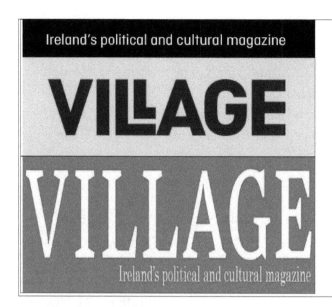

Ireland's political and cultural magazine

VILLAGE

VILLAGE

Ireland's political and cultural magazine

Village 18 August, 2014

Heaney: going through the poetic motions
Ireland's timeless bard of farmyard, bogs and prehistory
by Kevin Kiely

After his death last year the Independent newspaper described Séamus Heaney as "probably the best-known poet in the world". According to the BBC, at one time Heaney's books made up two-thirds of the sales of living poets in the UK. Séamus Heaney won a Nobel prize and every bauble imaginable but was it as much for his affable and erudite PERSONA as for his poetry or his insight?

Heaney immersed himself in a world of mythology and archaeology, finding his contemporary if anachronistic focus down on the farm, close by the sights and sounds of the bog.

The poetic method isn't great. For example in his totally famous poem, 'Digging', Heaney claims that his grandfather could cut more turf in a day "than any other man". This is his trademark: anecdotes chopped into lines of verse. But is it poetry?

In the same poem he views himself as unfit for farm work or turf cutting having only his pen, and concludes implausibly: 'I'll dig with it". The image does not work.

Though great poets must be particularly alive to the spirit of their times, Heaney's inspiration is not modern. In the introduction to his translation of the Anglo-Saxon epic Beowulf he admits his passion for "a nostalgia I didn't know I suffered until I experienced its fulfilment". This fulfilment saturates his final collection, The Human Chain set – characteristically – in the old familiar farmyard and prefaced with a workaday title poem about lifting grain on to a trailer "with a grip on two sack corners". Timeless perhaps, but searingly relevant to a traumatised post-industrial world, to an adolescent Ireland of abuse, corruption, pillage, Trouble – hardly.

It was not untypical that when Heaney finally decided to address the issue of the road proposed to dissect the ancient site of Tara, it was in the letters pages of the Irish Times. And too late, since a decision had already been taken. He never commented publicly on the destruction of the environment in the country he called home, which reached an uncosy, corrupted crescendo during his prime.

Heaney's poetry rarely leaves the farmstead for its subject matter. A Heaney poem entitled "Thatcher" will not be about politics. All of his pastoral work is nostalgic and anecdotal: "Churning Day" ; "The Forge"; "Gifts of Rain"; "Blackberry-Picking"; "Turkeys Observed"; "The Harrow-Pin" ; "Conkers" ; "The Seed Cutters" ; "Nostalgia in the Afternoon" ; "A Basket of Chestnuts"; "The Pitchfork"; "The Settle Bed"; "The Sandpit"; "Bog Oak"; "The Hill Farm"; "The Water Carrier"; "At A Potato Digging"; "The Gravel Walks"; "The Skylight"; "The Baler"; "Fireside" and "At the Wellhead". Heaney's obsession with the farm is about as broadening as a visit to an agricultural folklore museum.

The preoccupation with bogs was all-enveloping as he turned to bog corpses, skeletons and bones – all safely distancing him from the sectarian Troubles whose heinous burials of course find no resonance in Heaney. At base, Heaney is a poet of nostalgia for home, hearth, turf fire, hen-house and bicycle. His accessibility to readers equals that of Maeve Binchy whose chick-lit is if anything slightly more modern in content. The broadcasting equivalent is Miriam O'Callaghan (completely modern). He became everybody's favourite, famous Séamus. Everyséamus.

Approachability is Heaney's be-all. Last August, in a New York Times article, 'Another Kind of Music' on the day of Heaney's death, songwriter Paul Simon – the thoughtful half of Simon and Garfunkel ("Lie la lie, lie la lie la lie la, lie") – noted his "verbal virtuosity, his wit and Irish charm. Recovering from a stroke in the hospital, he greeted his friend and fellow poet Paul Muldoon with, "Hello, different strokes for different folks". One wonders how Simon or Muldoon would have coped with the verbal virtuosity, wit and Irish charm of an unwell Joyce or Beckett.

Heaney's lack of engagement with the Northern conflict was on display early on, in 'Summer 1969'. "While the Constabulary covered the mob/Firing into the Falls, I was suffering/Only the bullying sun of Madrid". The poem concludes with his retreating for the "cool of the Prado" to look at Goya's painting 'Shootings of the Third of May'. His empathy was that of the tourist.

His procrustean admirers explain that he was actually always obliquely engaging with the North. Heaney's best-known poem "Digging" ludicrously compares a pen to a gun to a shovel! It begins: 'Between my finger and my thumb/The squat pen rests; snug as a gun'. It's inaccurate, of course, in that a gun is not usually held between finger and thumb like a pen: a hand-gun has to be held using all fingers. However – after he had indeed toasted the queen – Heaney's most trenchant utterance came in 2013 and was surprisingly non-Nationalist for someone of his background: "There's never going to be a united Ireland. So why don't you let them [Loyalists] fly the flag?"

Bill Clinton serially, and nearly every cliché-unaware tout with a speech to make about the North and a message of political blandness, can be relied upon to marshal Heaney's phrase from Sophocles in translation that occasionally "hope and history rhyme". The poetry has became jingle before it acquired resonance, or even meaning. Heaney did world leaders and celebrities and was quite at home, for example in the Unicorn at a table of Clinton, Bono and twenty others, with Denis O'Brien picking up the tab, and – one imagines – private jets waiting at the airport for when the post-prandial brandies and payoff recitation had finally been discharged.

Séamus Deane, a direct peer of Heaney, wrote of him in the New Yorker in 2000 as having been from the beginning "'well in" with those in power – teachers, professors, and the like [but a]t the same time, he was conspiratorially against them, holding them at arm's length by his humour, his gift for parody [...] it was Heaney's way of dealing with his own contradictory sense of himself: his authority and his uncertainty. The balance between these was not delicate". Nor did it get more delicate with age.

Heaney's profile as a poet spawned his persona as Ireland's smile-eyed cultural minister without portfolio, led to posts in Harvard and Oxford, to awards including a Nobel Prize and to multifarious worthy endorsements. The academics, passive Eng. Litt. students and Booker-Prize novel-buyers felt securer reading Heaney because of his London publisher, Faber & Faber. Among academic critics who lavished praise on him, were Harold Bloom and Helen Vendler both of Harvard, John Carey of Oxford, and others such as poet Blake Morrison and collaborating academic Neil Corcoran. All of these were comfortable in following the American poet Robert Lowell's misguided high praise that Heaney was "the best Irish poet since Yeats". Lowell's editorial backer was TS Eliot, justly acknowledged as THE supreme modernist poet and founding director of Faber & Faber. After Eliot's demise, Charles Monteith from Lisburn, County Down, a former London barrister, took over and reflected the taste in poetry of his milieu. Monteith was a friend of Louis MacNeice, also a Faberman as were Auden, Lowell, Berryman and Hughes who brought to Faber, albeit posthumously, the poetry of his legendary ex-wife, Sylvia Plath. Monteith's mission in the 1960s was to aggrandise Richard Murphy, a fellow Irish Oxonian of Monteith's and Heaney who would later haul into Faber one of his students at QUB, Paul Muldoon.

Monteith's 'finding' Heaney in the 1960s at the beginning of the Troubles proved to be good for business. Heaney had the unobvious Northman cachet but was with all decidedly a 'safe' poet. Monteith rushed out four collections in a decade followed by Selected Poems. There was the bonus of media coverage when Heaney went into permanent exile in Dublin in 1972 with a summer house in Wicklow while being flown about in the Faber helicopter on beaming poetry-reading tours. Heaney's wife Marie Heaney, née Devlin sister of Barry Devlin of Horslips, ensured an easy entrée to RTÉ's arts programming.

Heaney was now sticking with his farmyard themes and continually ploughed the same furrow even in later collections with mawkish titles: Field Work, The Haw Lantern and Opened Ground. With a recommendation from Professor John L Sweeney Harvard reeled him in and Oxford soon followed by teeing up the Professorship of Poetry. His apotheosis as Nobel Laureate conjured an assured brand name in poetry: Famous Séamus Heaney.

To criticise Heaney's poetry is not permitted, and to do so in company is usually disapproved of as a definitive indication of being officially untutored. Mainstream reviewers – and who would not wish to be among them? – as well as academic journals dare not speak out against his work. Two analytical essays break the rule: Desmond Fennell's 'Whatever You Say, Say Nothing' (1991) and James Simmons' 'The Trouble with Séamus' (1992). When Éamon Dunphy criticised Heaney as "a sham national poet" in 1995 in The Sunday Independent he was seen as attacking a sacred cow. Indeed inevitably Heaney has the appropriate poem in praise of bovine pregnancy, "Cow in calf". And Dunphy recanted on his death (Heaney's).

A Nobel-winning poet propelled by a tide of charm, fashion and politics, he never rivalled Shaw, Yeats, Joyce or Beckett. Heaney's Nobel acceptance speech lacked rigour: "I credit poetry, in other words, both for being itself and for being a help…I credit it because credit is due to it, in our time and in all time, for its truth to life, in every sense of that phrase". This clearly reveals Heaney's shallowness of poetic insight. The sentiment is weak and the analysis is circular and otiose, that poetry is always merited because of its truth-to-life factor! "When a poem rhymes, when a form generates itself, when a metre provokes consciousness into new postures, it is already on the side of life. When a rhyme surprises and extends the fixed relations between words that in itself protests against necessity. When language does more than enough, as it does in all achieved poetry, it opts for the condition of overlife, and rebels at limit. The vision of reality which poetry offers should be transformative, more than just a printout of the given circumstances of its time and place". But is Heaney's lifey analysis not ultimately guff: what is his protest against necessity, what transformation did he seek?

Posterity will be the ultimate judge. Popular reputations fade. Poetic oblivion is a purgatory haunted by once over-rated literary reputations including those of William Allingham, Padraic Colum, James Stephens, and among British poets laureate (Heaney turned down the accolade), Robert Southey, Alfred Austin, John Masefield and Cecil Day-Lewis. Thomas Moore and Robert Burns are lately rated not even as poets but as song-writers (like Dylan and Morrissey). Paul Simon told the New York Times: "Songwriters have melody, instrumentation and rhythm to color their work and give it power; poets accomplish it all with words. Séamus, though, was one of those rare poets whose writing evokes music: the fiddles, pipes and penny-whistles of his Northern Irish culture and upbringing." Wrong, except for those nostalgists who strive to find penny whistles in every corner of this Emerald Isle. Heaney had no songs. Nor is he quotable, as evidenced in the obituaries that yawningly rehashed the most predictable lines from 'Digging' (cited below).

Did anyone ever try digging with a pen? It would go no deeper than the topsoil and leave no long-term legacy. The worry would be it was merely – the worst of all artistic sins – going through the motions.

Bill Clinton (left) enduring Heaney's nice-guy persona.

Seamus Heaney *New Selected Poems 1966-1987; New Selected Poems 1988-2013* (Faber & Faber).

This commissioned review was submitted to the Literary Editor of the *Irish Independent*

Heaney was a poet of nostalgia for home and hearth, the turf-fire, the hen house and the bicycle. With the farmyard as subject matter his poems are like exhibit notes in any agricultural museum. Heaney's accessibility compared well to Maeve Binchy whose chick-lit was slightly more modern in content.

In 'Exposure' he admitted having moved to Wicklow in 1972 and 'escaped from the massacre' in the North. He adopted mythology and archaeology. This preoccupation distanced him from the sectarian war. 'I found it more convincing to write about the bodies in the bog and the vision of Iron Age punishment'.

Heaney was always repressed and reticent about the North as in "Summer 1969". 'While the Constabulary covered the mob/Firing into the Falls, I was suffering/Only the bullying sun of Madrid.' It concludes with his retreating for the 'cool of the Prado' to look at Goya's painting 'Shootings of the Third of May'. This pretence to sympathy while on holiday, cooling off in exotic cities and protecting your own hide was typical of his lazy political content. Thus a Heaney poem entitled "Thatcher" is not about politics.

He was fond of anecdotes chopped into lines. But is it poetry? His great flaw is 'a nostalgia I didn't know I suffered until I experienced its fulfilment'. He stated this in the introduction to the Anglo-Saxon epic *Beowulf* which is extracted among the *New Selected Poems* in two volumes.

Heaney's verse is swamped in nostalgia like his titles: "Churning Day" ; "The Forge" ; "Gifts of Rain" ; "Blackberry-Picking" ; "Turkeys Observed" ; "The Harrow-Pin" ; "Conkers" ; "The Seed

Cutters" ; "Nostalgia in the Afternoon" ; "A Basket of Chestnuts" ; "The Pitchfork" ; "The Settle Bed" ; "The Sandpit" ; "Bog Oak" ; "The Hill Farm" ; "The Water Carrier" ; "At A Potato Digging" ; "The Gravel Walks" ; "The Skylight" ; "The Baler" ; "Fireside" and "At the Wellhead".

Solely because of Heaney's London publisher, Faber & Faber many 'uneducated' academics felt secure in praising him, including Harold Bloom and Helen Vendler both of Harvard, John Carey of Oxford, and others such as Blake Morrison, Neil Corcoran & Karl Miller. They supported the American poet Robert Lowell's misguided remark that Heaney was 'the best Irish poet since Yeats.' Lowell's backer was T. S. Eliot *the* supreme modernist poet and founding-director of Faber & Faber. After Eliot's death, Charles Monteith from Lisburn, County Down reflected a taste in verse from his milieu as former London barrister. Monteith's mission at Faber in the 1960s aimed at sustaining their illustrious legacy of poets such as Lowell, Louis MacNeice, W. H. Auden, John Berryman, Ted Hughes and Sylvia Plath. Monteith decided to publish fellow Oxonian, Richard Murphy and Heaney, who later recommended to Faber a student of his at QUB, Paul Muldoon.

Monteith's 'finding' Heaney was good for business because the North of Ireland dominated the media. Heaney was decidedly a 'safe' farmyard-themed, bog-themed poet. Monteith rushed out four books over a decade followed by the *Selected Poems.* Heaney continually ploughed the same furrow in subsequent collections reflecting his folkloric submersion: *Field Work, The Haw Lantern* and *Opened Ground.* The Nobel Prize made him a brand name: *Famous Seamus* coined by the TV critic, Clive James.

To criticise Heaney's poetry is not acceptable. Those who have dared to, such as Desmond Fennell in "Whatever You Say, Say Nothing" (1991) and James Simmons in "The Trouble with Seamus" (1992) were seen to be attacking a sacred cow. Heaney of course wrote a poem in praise of bovine pregnancy, titled "Cow in calf". The protective Heaney mafia endeavour to maintain his reputation as that of an untouchable demagogue. Despite his image as cultural icon, he never reached the achievements in literature of Wilde, Shaw, Yeats, Joyce and Beckett. His work is definitely not major.

Heaney's best-known poem "Digging" compares a pen to a gun to a shovel. As usual his mealy-mouthed heavy handed metaphors are to the fore. It begins: 'Between my finger and my thumb/The squat pen rests; snug as a gun'. This is inaccurate. A gun is not held between finger and thumb like a pen. A hand-gun is held properly using all fingers. Heaney claims in the poem that his grandfather could cut more turf in a day 'than any other man'. This is his standard trademark of anecdotes dull as ditchwater. "Digging" declares that he, Heaney as poet is unfit for farm-work or turf cutting, having only his pen, he concludes: 'I'll dig with it.' The poem is a ludicrous farce. You write with a pen, shoot with a gun and dig with a spade. For someone born on a farm was he pretending to be the simpleton? However, posterity usually means oblivion for such poets and is no respecter of academies, honours, awards, reputations and one-time mass popular praise. Who reads Robert Southey, Alfred Austin, John Masefield, Cecil Day-Lewis, William Allingham and James Stephens? It's quite simple: real poetry endures.

Heaney's final collection *The Human Chain* was set in his old familiar farmyard, saturated in mawkish descriptions amidst the usual wistful longings. The title poem is about lifting grain onto a trailer 'with a grip on two sack corners'. His first ever published poem was entitled 'Tractors'. Among his final pieces is 'Banks of a Canal' which begins: 'Say "canal" and there's that final vowel/Towing silence with it, slowing time.' Any lines at random show him up as self-consciously drawing attention to language in melodramatic tones somewhat similar to *Old Moore's Almanac* verse.

"Digging for the real worth of Seamus Heaney"

Review of Heaneys Collected Poems (Two Volumes) in the *Irish Independent*.

Kevin Kiely offers a possibly controversial view of the Nobel Prize-winning poet

09/11/2014

Heaney: sheepish verse-man

After his death last year, the London Independent newspaper described Seamus Heaney as "probably the best-known poet in the world". According to the BBC, Heaney's books of poetry at one time made up two-thirds of the sales of all living poets in the UK.

His success and reputation were legendary not only in Britain where his publisher had him flown about in a helicopter on poetry reading tours. By the 1980s he was regularly on call as visiting professor at Harvard University (1985-97) and at the same time professor of poetry at Oxford (1989-1994). The following year (1995), he received the Nobel Prize for literature.

Here at home, that award gave him a status unmatched by any other living writer, whether poet or novelist. It turned him into a national icon. He became Famous Seamus, a cross between a national treasure and a global guru. The twinkling eyes and the ever-smiling face, which somehow always remained inscrutable, gave him an aura of immense wisdom.

All this led many people, from presidents to plumbers, to his poetry. And that has to be a good thing. But fame is not the measure of how good a poet is and now, a year after his death, it is time for a more objective assessment. This is also made appropriate by the publication this week of his *New Selected Poems 1988-2013* and the republication in a matching hardback of his earlier volume, *New Selected Poems 1966-1987*.

Together, the two volumes give us Heaney's personal selection from his life's work, the poems he regarded as his best. If these are the best poems he produced, then his reputation must stand or fall on them.

It is this reviewer's opinion that it is high time for a new assessment of Heaney, not least because his work has also influenced Irish poetry. For better or worse, is the question. And there are many questions about the poet, the poetry and the reputation that need objective assessment.

Above all, Heaney was a poet of nostalgia for home and hearth, the turf-fire, the hen house and the bicycle. With the farmyard as subject matter, his poems are like exhibit notes in an agricultural museum. One of the results of this was to give his work an accessibility that compared well to Maeve Binchy, although her popular fiction was slightly more modern in content.

Another fundamental aspect of Heaney's appeal was that although he was a poet from Northern Ireland who was writing during the Troubles, he managed to keep his distance from the sectarian horror, like most of his readers. Instead he adopted mythology and archaeology. He chose to write about ancient bog bodies rather than the more recent burials in Northern bogs of the bodies of victims of the "war".

In "Exposure" he admitted having moved to Wicklow in 1972 and "escaped from the massacre" in the North. His preoccupation with pre-history and bogs distanced him from the sectarian war. "I found it more convincing to write about the bodies in the bog and the vision of Iron Age punishment".

Heaney was always repressed and reticent about the North, as in "Summer 1969". "While the Constabulary covered the mob/Firing into the Falls, I was suffering/Only the bullying sun of Madrid." That poem concludes with his retreating for the "cool of the Prado" to look at Goya's painting *Shootings of the Third of May*. This pretence to sympathy while on holiday, cooling off in exotic cities, was typical of his lazy political content. Thus a Heaney poem entitled "Thatcher" is not about politics.

As far as the writing itself is concerned, his poetic method isn't great. He was fond of anecdotes chopped into lines. But is it poetry? His great flaw is "a nostalgia I didn't know I suffered until I experienced its fulfilment." He stated this in the introduction to the Anglo-Saxon epic Beowulf which is extracted among the *New Selected Poems*.

Heaney's verse is swamped in nostalgia, like his titles: "Churning Day"; "The Forge"; "Gifts of Rain"; "Blackberry-Picking"; "Turkeys Observed"; "The Harrow-Pin"; "Conkers"; "The Seed Cutters"; "Nostalgia in the Afternoon"; "A Basket of Chestnuts"; "The Pitchfork"; "The Settle Bed"; "The Sandpit"; "Bog Oak"; "The Hill Farm"; "The Water Carrier"; "At a Potato Digging"; "The Gravel Walks"; "The Skylight"; "The Baler"; "Fireside" and "At the Wellhead."

Solely because of the reputation of Heaney's London publisher, Faber & Faber, many academics felt secure in praising him, like Harold Bloom of Harvard, John Carey of Oxford, and others such as Blake Morrison. They supported the American poet Robert Lowell's misguided remark that Heaney was "the best Irish poet since Yeats." Lowell's backer was TS Eliot, the supreme modernist poet and founding-director of Faber & Faber.

After Eliot's death, Charles Monteith from Lisburn, Co Down, took over the helm at Faber and reflected a taste in verse from his milieu as a former London barrister. Monteith's mission at Faber in the 1960s aimed at sustaining their illustrious legacy of poets such as Lowell, Louis MacNeice, W. H. Auden, John Berryman, Ted Hughes and Sylvia Plath. Monteith decided to publish fellow Oxonian Richard Murphy and Heaney.

Monteith's "finding" Heaney was good for business because the North was dominating the media. Heaney was decidedly a "safe" poet. Monteith rushed out four books over a decade. Heaney continually ploughed the same furrow in subsequent collections reflecting his folkloric submersion: *Field Work*, *The Haw Lantern* and *Opened Ground*. The Nobel Prize made him a brand name: Famous Seamus, coined by the TV critic Clive James.

To criticise Heaney's poetry is not yet acceptable in academic circles. Those who have dared to, such as Desmond Fennell in

"Whatever You Say, Say Nothing" (1991) and James Simmons in "The Trouble with Seamus" (1992), have been attacked, as though they were trying to kill a sacred cow. (Heaney, of course, wrote a poem in praise of bovine pregnancy, titled "Cow in Calf.") The Heaney mafia fiercely protect his reputation. But despite his position as cultural icon, the fact is he never reached the achievements in literature of Wilde, Shaw, Yeats, Joyce and Beckett. His work is definitely not major.

An example of Heaney's less than impressive ability with words is his best-known poem "Digging", which compares a pen to a gun to a shovel. As usual his mealy-mouthed, heavy-handed metaphors are to the fore. It begins: "Between my finger and my thumb/The squat pen rests; snug as a gun." This is simply inaccurate. A gun is not held between finger and thumb like a pen. A hand-gun is held properly using all fingers.

Heaney claims in the poem that his grandfather could cut more turf in a day "than any other man." This is his standard trademark of anecdotes, frequently dull as ditchwater. "Digging" declares that he, Heaney, as a poet is unfit for farm work or turf cutting, having only his pen. He concludes: "I'll dig with it."

The poem is both simplistic and contrived. You write with a pen, shoot with a gun and dig with a spade. As someone born on a farm, he should have known the difference.

Posterity is no respecter of academies, honours, awards, reputations and one-time mass popular praise. These days, who reads Robert Southey, Alfred Austin, John Masefield, Cecil Day-Lewis, William Allingham and James Stephens? It's quite simple: real poetry endures. Posterity decides.

Heaney's first-ever published poem was entitled "Tractors." His final collection *Human Chain* was set in his old familiar farmyard, saturated in mawkish descriptions amidst the usual wistful longings. The title poem is about lifting grain on to a trailer "with a grip on two sack corners." Among his final pieces is "Banks of a Canal" which begins: "Say 'canal' and there's that final vowel/Towing silence with it, slowing time." These lines show him up as self-consciously drawing attention to language in melodramatic tones somewhat similar to Old Moore's Almanac verse.

All this may seem harsh. But at this stage corrective views are essential if we are to begin to assess Heaney's real worth as a poet. Some digging is required.

Sheep-headed bard, and the Norn pantheon

Observe the Poe-Heads of Ulster marching towards Faber & Faber

Kevin Kiely

I give you two fingers in a definite V for victory
This art thrives on excellence: not wet-turf stack poetry
I could never dig with Seamus's sheep-shaped head
And between forefinger and thumb hold a laptop instead

These careerist Norn Iron poets hijacked language to build a lego-fake
Hyped up rural idolatry parading as literary earthquake
While Charlie Monteith fawned on the London Literary Press via Faber & Faber
British guilt exalted a daisy chain of re-verse-men smudging on Paper & Paper
Frog-marching poeds cashed-in as civil rights fought wrongs in the North
Alone: the real suffering people linked broken arms and marched forth

In a dirty tricks fix vacuous movement of empty mouth
Akin to many of the mushroom-dolmen presses in the South
Fitted green carpet-poets finding a slim volume audience at home
Nostalgia for farm, kitchen, pigsty, and the sub-Kavanagh bog-longing poem

Imagine bleating sheep dressed in homespun ill-fitting woolly kilts
And dull little po-hems like turf-smoke signals, basically: stilted verse on stilts
But this cunning clique worked up a jumble of politics to blame and shame us
And a pretence to proxy history while their aim was fame and be famous
They made ideal Media fillers betwixt the Troubles and Full Page Ads
A bunch of self-exiled, non-artistic have-nots and talentless-never-hads
Rising on the sectarian tide, implying they were speaking for their people
As they pumped up their Plastic Paddy Parnassian Folkloric steeple
Parading dialect as a hallmark: yet, overtly steeped in political journalese
Fooling many with their coughs and preambles and non-literature-tease
Nothing more than a crinkle suited hackademic phalanx pulling strings
Through insider institutional congregational readings
Keeping their bleary dreary eyes on the Guardian, TLS and the BBC
London, Boston, New York, the Irish Times and RTÉ

These pretender dumb-pome-men with exported clipped tones
Poe-Biz behind the scenes and bookings on the phones
Ambassadorial culture-salesfolk who traded IN their native NI
Hotly pursuing reputations for which they would die
Rather than spend a week in Belfast, Armagh or Derry
Unless with a film crew, taxis, and dinners preceded by Tio Pepe Fino sherry
These were the dry-wall poet-spoofs, truly northern, truly rooted
Never beaten, jailed, bombed out, harassed or hooted
Living safely and squarely in Southern Ireland vainly and gainly
Writing North of North about its pastoral landscape mainly
Metaphor gone mad, slack cadenced vocality of the locality
A poetry of fauna, flora and the threshing machine's practicality

These were a Fallacy all in one queue:
Paulin & Murphy & Mahon & Montague
Heaney & Longley & Bugaboo Muldoon
Inhabiting their Shangri-La-La Land
North by North of Pseudo-Brigadoon
Frauds posing with putrid books in hand
Soft-slippered yodellers out of tune

Never exposed for being right royal hypocrites
Poking poetry-hams at home, at America and at peace-loving mainland Brits
Ireland's self-styled scribe-heroes spewing fashionable green ink
Of ploughs, potatoes, hayforks, yokel-clichés and the jawbox sink
Pulling a fast one with nod and wink
Smarter than their public don't you think
They connived, cajoled and curried favour
These cowards abandoned their next door neighbour
And are outed here for their Caper & Caper
Observe that the poe-headers of Ulster marched towards Faber & Faber

May 2016 **s** **3**

Commissioned Poem from *VILLAGE magazine: politics and culture*

Observe the Poe-Heads of Ulster marching towards Faber & Faber

Kevin Kiely

I give you two fingers in a definite V for victory

This art thrives on excellence: not wet-turf stack poetry

I could never dig with Seamus's sheep-shaped head

And between forefinger and thumb hold a laptop instead

These careerist Norn Iron poets hijacked language to build a lego-fake

Hyped up *rural idolatry parading as literary earthquake*

While Charlie Monteith fawned on the London Literary Press via Faber & Faber

British guilt exalted a daisy chain of re-verse-men smudging on Paper & Paper

Frog-marching poeds cashed-in as civil rights fought wrongs in the North

Alone: the real suffering people linked broken arms and marched forth

In a dirty tricks fix vacuous movement of empty mouth

Akin to many of the mushroom-dolmen presses in the South

Fitted green carpet-poets finding a slim volume audience at home

Nostalgia for farm, kitchen, pigsty, and the sub-Kavanagh bog-longing poem

Imagine bleating sheep dressed in homespun ill-fitting woolly kilts

And dull little po-hems like turf-smoke signals, basically: stilted verse on stilts

But this cunning clique worked up a jumble of politics to blame and shame us

And a pretence to proxy history while their aim was fame and be famous

They made ideal Media fillers betwixt the Troubles and Full Page Ads

A bunch of self-exiled, non-artistic have-nots and talentless-never-hads

Rising on the sectarian tide, implying they were speaking for their people

As they pumped up their Plastic Paddy Parnassian Folkloric steeple

Parading dialect as a hallmark: yet, overtly steeped in political journalese

Fooling many with their coughs and preambles and non-literature-tease

Nothing more than a crinkle suited hackademic phalanx pulling strings

Through insider institutional congregational readings

Keeping their bleary dreary eyes on the Guardian, TLS and the BBC

London, Boston, New York, the Irish Times and RTÉ

These pretender dumb-pome-men with exported clipped tones

Poe-Biz behind the scenes & bookings on the phones

Ambassadorial culture-salesfolk who traded IN their native NI

Hotly pursuing reputations for which they would die

Rather than spend a week in Belfast, Armagh or Derry

Unless with a film crew, taxis, and dinners preceded by *Tio Pepe Fino* sherry

These were the dry-wall poet-spoofs, truly northern, truly rooted

Never beaten, jailed, bombed out, harassed or hooted

Living safely and squarely in Southern Ireland vainly and gainly

Writing North of North about its pastoral landscape mainly

Metaphor gone mad, slack cadenced vocality of the locality

A poetry of fauna, flora and the threshing machine's practicality

These were a Fallacy all in one queue:

Paulin & Murphy & Mahon & Montague

Heaney& Longley & Bugaboo Muldoon

Inhabiting their Shangri-La-La Land

North by North of Pseudo-Brigadoon

Frauds posing with *putrid books* in hand

Soft-slippered yodelers out of tune

Never exposed for being right royal hypocrites

Poking *poetry-hams* at home, at America and at *peace-loving* mainland Brits

Ireland's self-styled scribe-heroes spewing fashionable green ink

Of ploughs, potatoes, hayforks, yokel-clichés and the jawbox sink

Pulling a fast one with nod and wink

Smarter than their public don't you think

They connived, cajoled and curried favour

These cowards abandoned their next door neighbour

And are outed here for their Caper & Caper

Observe that the poe-headers of Ulster marched towards Faber & Faber

First published in *Café Review* (USA), *New ::: Poetry* (International), and *VILLAGE: politics and culture* (Ireland)

Afterword: Heaney's toxic cult

As a poetry critic for *Hibernia* in the 1970s, the editor John Mulcahy published my first review. I had been sent various collections of poems by Peter Regrove, Brendan Kennelly and a Heaney/Derek Mahon pamphlet *In their Element*. I'd better state that at the time my poems were only, if at all permitted into poetry magazines, and very few at that, but what poetry of mine was 'known' gained me a position as critic on the fortnightly publication *Hibernia*.

In their Element was a British Arts Council publication which I stewed over, and it represented the first four H-collections which I immediately recognised as not being 'poetry'. I have reviewed Mahon's *Collected Poems* and refrain from quoting it here. The pamphlet *In their Element*, I vividly recall left me aghast and frustrated as one is at the age of twenty-four with what was being trumpeted as 'poetry'; especially as my travels in poetry had really propelled me well beyond the contemporary Irish scene.

I railed against such verses, and among them "Digging" which seemed to me such a travesty of what even good doggerel might be or comic verse or song, anything but H's little squibs barely filling the centre of most pages. "Digging" was being approved as contemporaneously 'Northern' as if a Renaissance hailed from there reflecting the sectarian war. Therefore, H must be important because there was mention of a gun in the verse. The use of 'gun' in "Digging" I have publicly shown-up in *VILLAGE* and the *Irish Independent* and in reply to the pro-H furore and personal insults thrown my way over speaking out for real poetry as opposed to his version. At the time I first read it, "Digging" was being cunningly utilised as sound bite to make H as the ideal pacifist but anyone who lived in or around Ireland (1968-1998) even temporarily knew that war means taking sides. There is no neutrality about the North of Ireland Sectarian War while the peace process more than twenty years on leaves much unfinished business concerning the unresolved

Irish Question which requires one urgent obvious solution: if London's Westminster, for once in their imperial history will present humanity and not their perennial evil actions towards Ireland.

I couldn't approve of H's "Digging" when I quickly realised that it was such a genre of counterfeit that would make my own situation as a poet 'difficult' faced with this school of fraudulence. The situation was serious, as some of my contemporaries voiced dissenting views as my own but it was largely an Arts Council monetarily controlled scene, and many felt that the gravy came before gravitas. Poetry was actually being excluded.

Anyway, I set too, and wrote a review of Redgrove, Kennelly and *In their Element*, and sent it to Mulcahy, the editor. Some weeks later, I received a letter in gratitude from Brendan Kennelly. *Hibernia* was 'unable to print my review because it dealt unfavourably with H' who also occasionally reviewed fellow Irish poets and even Ted Hughes with loud praise. There seemed to be a single reviewing method for H: praise, praise, praise, and protect your own forthcoming collections a definite tit for tat: scratch my back and I will scratch yours. The other rule was whoever publishes the most collections before they die: wins. In Ireland that meant courting the state sponsored poetry publishers whose 'owners' were 'poets' themselves and their advisors but I have discussed this situation in a series of articles, already published and must get on with my own work in poetry.

Back then, my voice had to be silenced as being a dissenting one. I was soon *ex-Hibernia*. Forty years later, my appraisal remains the same, except that when commissioned to write about H for *Village* and the national broadsheet *The Irish Independent* I was literally appalled in revisiting his *Collected Poems* over two volumes. I presently register that H is devoid of any ability except the weakest minimum as minor verse maker: so multitudinous are his imperfections as a writer that I apologise to the genuine reader for having to plunge through the dirge of his stuff. His clique of clones have disserved Irish poetry and left it internationally seen as minor stuff of a homogenous H-genre.

I cannot recall what I wrote at the time for *Hibernia* but it lost me my reviewer's job as a young man, and more importantly as a poet but I prevailed amidst a heinous and venal era. I was repelled by the 'poems' and the blurb that stated 'Heaney's poetry emerges from the sedimentary process, Mahon's from the igneous'. I noticed on locating the pamphlet in the Linen Hall Library, Belfast recently that there are no page numbers. The blurb is meaningless.

Thus his so-called poems are glossed and critically dismissed: you can't change H's squalid verses, nor ever can, so I state that time and history will deal with them justly, but let me be clear: they will not last, nor gain further audience where real poetry holds its domain. I had a similar experience in writing about the 'poetry' of the Irish President, Michael D. Higgins and was subjected to defamation in the press and media and in the aftermath of reviewing H's verses, losing my position as *Poetry Reviewer* for the very journal in which I had reviewed Higgins. Thus the establishment of H and his octopus clique that prop up the great poetry hoax. If H wasn't held in such esteem by the poetry establishment then such as President Higgins wouldn't presume to be a poet. But I am free to write and await my next and forthcoming poems, for Ireland is not quite fully culturally totalitarian, however, it does harbour many controlling cliques and cabals. I must return to my poems, for the critic is ever guilty of neglecting the primal urge, forever in a lover's quarrel with poetry and its emissaries.

Among many occasions, when I was depressed by this situation and especially when among two other 'poems' handed out in a tutorial in UCD in the 1970s, were two of H's. There were of course, other choices of real poetry offered, but in the nature of student days, one had to toe the line, and turn in commentary, known as *Practical*

Criticism on assigned poetry. My teacher was a notable international professor, and in fact part of the cultural milieu that dictated what was 'poetry'. Augustine Martin had edited the Leaving Certificate Anthology *Soundings*, yes, a dreadful title which I reviewed in *Inis* Summer 2011 since it had been re-issued in a nostalgic edition, for it did purvey more than a limited miscellany of contemporary Irish consensus poetry. Professor 'Gus' as he was known had provided in *Soundings* the equivalent of a High-School or A-Level poetry syllabus that was not undesirable, including Milton, Shakespeare, Eliot, Dickinson, Yeats and others, and became a canonical primer for decades in schools. It could not satisfy my needs for very long but still it was not totally redundant.

My objections at college level were almost unacceptable to Professor Augustine Martin, whom I pursued after the tutorial, demanding to know if he really thought that "Digging" was actually poetry or the other verse, "Docker". My ire was, that 'Gus' had compared "Docker" as a caricature of an Orangeman, (basically a sectarian bigot) to Yeats's "The Fisherman". To my satisfaction, Gus agreed that H's poem was only 'like' the Yeats's poem in being a character-depiction poem, and certainly no-where near as good as Yeats's. At least he admitted this and I felt some satisfaction.

I wanted to know if Gus thought that the H poems were poetry? He replied that I was free to choose what poems and poets to write about, and to express why I disliked certain poems. I could even avoid the H poems, *if they were that offensive to my sensibility*. He was being his usual avuncular self, and always maintained amicable professor-student relationships: he was accessible and discursive within his own parameters. My preferences were decidedly American and European, but I could hardly endure much of the post-1960s Irish poetry. I dogmatically stick by my opinion that it was a poisonous era, largely for reasons stated elsewhere, but I have reviewed shards of the output, in as much as I could face the task as critic.

Anyway, Gus finally, in order to escape an impassioned student and young poet, yielded as he waited for the elevator. 'Look,' he said as the fanlight blinked and the elevator slowly chugged from the ground floor to the English Department, 'Heaney will probably write far better poetry. It is early days, yet. I agree, the two I choose for the tutorial are pretty basic. They are slim poems. Alright? You should read only what absorbs you fully, therefore ignore H as if he didn't exist for you as a poet. As he obviously doesn't [...]'. At this point, the elevator doors had joined on Gus, and I as solitary student felt somewhat satisfied that day in the English Faculty.

But, of course H went on and on, in Favour & Favour (Faber & Faber) and among those who pushed his sophistry and rhetoric of the farmyard as the anecdotal sloppy sentimental childhood garden of his verses. As I write, the statistics for the year's farming fatal accidents has featured farmers who find nothing sentimental in the dirt, rain, and endless labour of farm work.

Besides, A. N. Wilson, Anthony Burgess, Carol Rumens, Andrew Waterman, John Bayley, Tom Herron, Desmond Fennell, James Simmons and others have voiced and printed their critiques, and thus making them ethical more than those who voiced them over faculty-coffee to me, and disappeared into the photocopy room to reproduce H and H from F&F.

However, and to conclude my task; in 2013 (partially related at the start of this book), I found myself on the organising committee of The International Ezra Pound Society who had voted to have their bi-annual conference in Dublin. I could give the names of those who invited H as plenary guest speaker but there were other plenary speakers. H accepted and duly arrived delivering his lecture on Pound or more accurately, 20-30 minute asides of comments with quotations from the *Pisan Cantos* so well known and buttressed by no argument or discourse, and received politely, if impatiently. Conference papers are predominantly ground-breaking or meant to be whereas H and his bygone metaphors and rural sayings was quite a failure.

I better admit to meeting H at lunch in the campus corridor location, such is the norm as conferences demand schedules that run to time. H was his public diplomatic self with pounds of praise for the scholarly learning and discourse. All of it, so above him which made me think what kind of papers would this bunch have delivered on "Digging" and other verses. Besides, to my delight I noticed that the academics—an international throng—had not invited H to give a poetry reading. In 2013, surely, if he was rated as by his admirers, these Poundians would have wanted him to grace the conference with a reading (Lord protect us!). Instead they only required him as thirty-minute mascot and indeed there was a poetry reading. I gave a poetry reading with others.

The alert poetry reader will understand why I classify H as the Daniel O'Donnell of Irish Literature. H's adoration of Robert Frost may be roughly compared to O'Donnell's adoration of Loretta Lynn and how his dream came true when they performed together in his home village of Kincasslagh, County Donegal. '[...] that she actually visited me in my village' (DOD 7). O'Donnell's work for charity is as famous as his crooning, but no one should mock or belittle the great generosity of this life, including his deeply charitable development of the Romanian Orphanage Appeal (DOD 121) as well as the joy he brings his fans.

O'Donnell sings from a ballad, pop, and country repertoire known to millions. When H is compared to O'Donnell it is in terms of their shared space with regard to rural country and western tropes already over-done and the fall-back of basic bygone nostalgia. You can relate many of H's titles to the O'Donnell songs that his fan base

150

enjoy while in actual fact there are many similarities between the songs and H's content: "Veil of White Lace"; "Medals for Mothers"; "Pat Murphy's Meadow"; "A Letter from the Postman's Bag"; "Never Be Anyone Else But You"; "Little Cabin Home on the Hill"; "I Heard the Bluebirds Sing"; "Footsteps"; "In the Garden"; "Even On Days That It Rained"; "Yesterday's Memories"; "These Are My Mountains"; "Ramblin' Rose"; "The Blackthorn Stick"; "Put Your Hand In The Hand Of A Man"; "Homeland"; "Our House Is A Home" and "Shoe The Donkey".

Therefore finally, I resort to use 'moral' and use it akin to ethical, and point to the injustice of forcing H's verse upon unsuspecting student-readers from the ages of 8-18, and beyond. I would deny no-one the right to read what they want, but I present this book as evidence that H's product is not poetry. H was a pushed Faber product and a great poetry hoax, in other words not poetry. Why read such counterfeit when the real glory of real poetry is at hand, online and in print. If you think "Digging" is a 'poem' then read the parody of it below, and I trust you will conclude that both are ludicrous, imprecise, volatile, melodramatic exercises in chopped lines spuriously posing as 'poems'. Do you really wish to involve yourself with the fake and the counterfeit, with a paper moon when the real thing is available, with a scribbled sun on a page when there are myriads of real suns? I mean the real fire of poets and poetry. Not, the sort of diatribe "Digging" is and similar in diatribe to this parody:

Stirring

Non-Homage to S.H.

Between my finger and thumb

The spoon rests snug as a spoon.

Under my window, a clean scraping sound

When the spoon sinks into the tin mug.

It's my father stirring, I look down

Till his straining hand, elbow and spoon

Twisting and turning in the tea until

He has really sweetened it up

While he was stirring.

Ah the fingers holding his spoon, the shaft

Against the mug-side levered firmly.

He stirred up that tea, buried in sugar

To scatter the grains that he had scooped

Loving those grains, each little diamond bit.

By God, the old man could handle a spoon.

Just like his old man.

My grandfather spooned more sugar in a day

Than any other tea-drinker in Castledawson.

Once, I carried him milk in a bottle

Corked sloppily with paper. He straightened up:

'Oh Sheamus, did you forget the fuckin' sugar?'

Still he stirred the tea; heaving it down his throat

Glancing over his shoulder. 'No sugar! No sugar!

For the tea.' Nothing stirring.

The tea alone in its lonely tin-mug

Of tea, tea bereaved of sugar, sugarless.

This all awoke into my head in distress.

But I've no spoon to follow men like them.

Between my finger and thumb

The spoon rests

I'll stir with it.

Digging (excerpted)

By Seamus Heaney

Between my finger and my thumb

The squat pen rests; snug as a gun.

Under my window, a clean rasping sound

When the spade sinks into gravelly ground:

&&&&&

By God, the old man could handle a spade.

Just like his old man.

My grandfather cut more turf in a day

Than any other man on Toner's bog.

&&&&&

But I've no spade to follow men like them.

Between my finger and my thumb

The squat pen rests.

I'll dig with it.

Timeline: While the Sectarian War (1968-1998) raged on, H produced nostalgic collections and titles (listed below)

H's Faber & Faber books with year of publication.	The North of Ireland Sectarian War (selected incidents) vaguely referenced in few verses of H's Faber & Faber Collections.
1966: *Death of a Naturalist*	1966: Ulster Volunteer Force (UVF) heavily armed by Britain issue a statement declaring war on the Irish Republican Army (IRA). IRA celebrate the 1916 Rising which led to Ireland's Independence from Britain except for the 6 counties of the North. UVF killings begin with three civilians murdered.
1969: *Door into the Dark*	1969: People's Democracy March (Nationalists seeking Human Rights) attacked by Loyalists and RUC (the Six Counties Police Force) while passing through Burntollet returning to Derry. 'Battle of the Bogside'; Riots in Bogside when RUC and Loyalists attack Nationalists. Westminster Government send British Troops in the Six Counties.
1972: *Wintering Out*	1972: Bloody Sunday in Derry, 13 Civilians shot dead by British Soldiers during an anti-Internment-without-Trial March.
1975: *North*	1975: Miami Showband

	Massacre by Loyalists; 'Shankill Butchers Gang' begin their random cut-throat murders on Nationalists in Belfast.
1979: *Field Work*	1979: Loyalist 'Shankill Butchers Gang' of 11 cut-throats jailed.
1980: *Preoccupations*; *Poems 1965-1975*	1980: IRA Volunteers begin Hunger Strikes in the Maze Concentration Camp Prison during which Bobby Sands and nine others die having sought political status as prisoners under the Thatcher Government.
1982: H's Harvard University years begin (5 year contract)	1982: IRA London bombings.
1984: *Station Island*	1984: IRA Brighton Hotel bombing with Thatcher as prime target.
1987: *Haw Lantern*	1987: Loughgall 8 Provisional IRA volunteers killed and one civilian by British SAS. Enniskillen PIRA bombing 11 civilians and one RUC policeman killed.
1988: *Government of the Tongue*	1988: Loyalist Michael Stone kills 3 mourners in Milltown Cemetery (Belfast), SAS killing of 3 PIRA in Gibralter; Ballgawley (County Tyrone) Bus bomb kills 8 British Soldiers.
1990: *Selected Poems: 1966-1987*	London Stock Exchange Bombed.
1991: *Seeing Things*	Thatcher resigns as Dictator

	Prime Minister.
1995: *The Redress of Poetry*	British and Irish Government cooperate in Framework Document for peace in the Six Counties.
1996: *The Spirit Level*	Drumcree Conflict as Loyalists demand marching rights through Nationalist area causing riots.
2001: *Electric Light*	Decommissioning of IRA weapons. RUC replaced by the PSNI the 'new version/old version' police service in the 6 Counties.
2002: *Finders Keepers*	Holy Cross Catholic Girls' School in Belfast subjected to months of attacks from Loyalist protesters since 2001.
2006: *District and Circle*	Michael Stone (Loyalist murderer) arrested.
2010: *Human Chain*	International Arms Decommissioning Tribunal steps down as UDA and INLA de-activate weapons.

Bibliography

Abbreviations in square brackets after author and title

Eileen Battersby (2004): "A Greek tragedy for our times" *The Irish Times* 3rd April "Weekend". [Battersby]

Fran Brearton and Alan Gillis, *The Oxford Handbook of Modern Irish Poetry* Oxford University Press 2012. [Brearton and Gillis]

Brian Coffee, *Poems of Mallarmé* Bilingual Edition London/Dublin The Menard Press/New Writers' Press 1990. [Mallarmé]

Neil Corcoran, *The Poetry of Seamus Heaney: a critical study* Faber and Faber, 1998. [Corcoran]

Conor Cruise O'Brien, *Memoir: my life and themes* Dublin Poolbeg, 1998. [COB]

Daniel O'Donnell and Eddie Rowley, *Daniel O'Donnell: my story the official book* (revised and updated) O'Brien Press, 2003. [DOD]

Stephen Fry, *The Ode Less Travelled unlocking the poet within* Arrow Books, 2007. [Fry]

Lorna Hardwick, "Seamus Heaney's Burial at Thebes" *Arts Past and Present Cultural Encounters* ed. Richard Danson Brown The Open University, 2008. [Hardwick]

Henry Hart, *Seamus Heaney: poet of contrary progressions* Syracuse University Press, 1992. [Hart]

Seamus Heaney, *Beowulf: a new translation* Faber and Faber, 1999. [B]

---*A Bibliography 1959-2003* eds. Rand Brandes and Michael J. Durkan Faber and Faber, 2008. [BiB]

---,*The Burial at Thebes: Sophocles' Antigone* Faber and Faber, 2004. [Thebes]

---,*Finders Keepers: Selected Prose 1971-2001* Faber and Faber 2002. [FKeep]

---,*The Government of the Tongue: the 1986 T. S. Eliot Memorial Lectures and Other Critical Writings* Faber and Faber, 1988. [GOT]

---,*The Human Chain* Faber and Faber, 2010. [HC]

---*The Redress of Poetry* Faber and Faber, 1995. [RP]

---,*New Selected Poems 1988-2013* Faber and Faber, 2014. [NSP 88-13]

---, *New Selected Poems 1966-1987* Faber and Faber, 2014. [NSP 66-87]

---, *Opened Ground Poems 1966-1996* Faber and Faber, 1998. [OG]

---, *Seeing Things* Faber and Faber, 1991. [ST]

---. *The Spirit Level*, Faber & Faber, 1996. [SL]

---, *Stepping Stones* ed. Dennis O'Driscoll Faber & Faber, 2008. [StepStone]

David Johnson, ed. *The Popular and the Canonical* Oxfordshire: Routledge; Milton Keynes: The Open University 2005. [PopCan]

Dillon Johnston, *Irish Poetry After Joyce* 2nd Edition New York: Syracuse Press, 1997. [IPAJ]

Poetry of Robert Frost ed. Edward Connery Lathem London: Vintage 2001. [Frost]

James Joyce, *Ulysses* ed. Jeri Johnston Oxford University Press (World's Classics), 1993. [U]

Kevin Kiely, "Seamus Heaney Timeless Poet of Bogs" Village Magazine: politics and culture 18 August 2014 ; 54-6.

---, "Digging for the Real Worth of Seamus Heaney" Review of New Selected Poems 1966-1987 and New Selected Poems 1988-2013 in *Irish Independent Weekend Review* 9 November 2014; 22-3.

Thomas Kinsella, introd. *The New Oxford Book of Irish Verse* Oxford University Press, 1986. [Kinsella]

Karl Kirchwey, "To Hell and Back" review of Seamus Heaney *Aeneid Books VI: a new verse translation* 'Sunday Book Review': *The New York Times*; June 12, 2016; p. 20). [Kirch]

Kochanowski *Laments* Stanislaw Bananczak & Seamus Heaney Gallery Press, 2009.

Maeve McDonagh, *Freedom of Information Law* 3rd Edition (Thomson Reuters Ireland Ltd., 2015). [McDon]

William Oxley, ed. *Completing the Picture: exiles, outsiders and independents* Devon: UK, Stride Publications, 1995. [Ox]

Sylvia Plath, *Ariel* Faber & Faber, 1965. [Ariel]

Ezra Pound, *Literary Essays* ed. T. S. Eliot (New York: New Direction, 1968) 271. [EPLE]

James Robson in *Ideas of Authority* eds. Lynda Prescott and Fiona Richards Milton Keynes: Open University, 2014. [IA]

A Twentieth-Century Literature Reader: Texts and Debates eds. Suman Gupta & David Johnson, Routledge 2005; 268-9). [TD]

Neil Sammells, rev. of *"Seamus Heaney: A Collection of Critical Essays* by Elmer Andrews" *Critical Survey* Vol. 6, No. 2 (1994). [Sammells]

Helen Vendler, *Seamus Heaney* HarperCollins, 1998. [Vend]

Walt Whitman, The Portable Walt Whitman revis'd & enlarg'd ed. Mark van Doran Penguin, 1982. [WW]

William Butler Yeats: Yeats 150 ed. Declan J. Foley Lilliput, 2016. [Foley]

Acknowledgements

I am indebted to Michael Smith, Editor of *VILLAGE: politics and culture* for publishing my essay on Heaney, and indeed to John Spain, Books Editor of the *Irish Independent* in inviting me to review the *Collected Poems* (2 Vols) of Heaney. Both editors have my respect for furthering the universal standards of the Fourth Estate, and the absolute terms in Freedom of the Press & Media.

I am indebted for discussions about, and editing of the text, to Pamela Mary Brown.

Author's Editorial Note

I am giving my research here, according to the legal definition of 'a search or investigation undertaken to discover facts and reach new conclusions by the critical study of a subject' (McDon 638).

The character of usage required no single poem quoted in full while much of Heaney's work is available online at many sites, on YouTube and otherwise beyond print which renders it 'in the public domain'. The Poetry Foundation, Poemhunter.com also renders poems online into the public domain just as the copious Tom O'Bedlam's YouTube site does. The fact that the few lines minimal from any single poem quoted in the text are fully available online does not take from their original copyright holders as print publishers © Faber & Faber to whom I duly make acknowledgement and obeisance. I am complying with fair usage in presenting extracts and other brief quotations from H's works listed in the bibliography, along with scholarly readings from critical studies and published reviews.

In reiteration, I am claiming fair use of extracts within strategic usage, and, in the amount and substantiality of extracts the percentage of quotation is very low. Thus, there is no infringement commercially in using fair usage of extracts from any poem, and critical works on such poems.

Hereby, copyright in all extracts remains with their authors and publishers in whatever form; every in-text reference is located expertly, clearly, and to every original publication source. In the event of hyper-commercial gain through the first edition from Areopagitica, copyright infringements if presented by publishers and editors shall be addressed in full in subsequent editions; however these strictures are already addressed in the legalism of this Author's 'Editorial Note'. In its present form 'Seamus Heaney and the Great Poetry Hoax' does not infringe any copyright; to repeat: the in-text citations attest to all original publication sources for all works cited and fairly quoted in fair usage.

Photograph credits are copyright to their creators and from Bing's free public usage: copyright is with the makers but with the timelag may be out of copyright; if not, a future edition(s) will duly acknowledge any photographer and his/her work overlooked as to copyright.

NOTE ON THE AUTHOR

Kevin Kiely poet, novelist, literary critic, raconteur and American Fulbright Scholar gained his PhD in modernist and postmodernist poetry from University College Dublin. He was born in County Down (Northern Ireland) and has received six Arts Council Bursaries in Literature, a Kavanagh Fellowship in Poetry and a Bisto Award for Fiction.

He is an Honorary Fellow of the Iowa International Writing Programme, was visiting Professor of English in Boise State University and the University of Idaho (Moscow), and has taught Romantic Literature at UCD. His critical commentaries on poetry, the arts, and cultural issues have appeared in *Village Magazine*, *Hibernia, Irish Examiner, Irish Studies Review, Honest Ulsterman, Fortnight, Books Ireland, The London Magazine, The Irish Book Review, Poetry Ireland Review, Irish Times, The Irish Independent, Irish Arts Review, Inis, Irish Literary Review, Idaho Arts Quarterly* and *Humanities* (DC) among other publications.

Published titles include *Quintesse* (St Martin's Press, New York) 1985; Gavin Witt English Major Yale University wrote a study of *Quintesse*, 1988). *Mere Mortals* Poolbeg, Dublin 1989 (Short-List Hughes & Hughes Fiction Prize 1990). *A Horse Called El Dorado* (O'Brien Press, 2005) Bisto Award. *Breakfast with Sylvia* (Lagan Press, 2006) Patrick Kavanagh Fellowship Award. *Francis Stuart: Artist and Outcast*—Official Biography (Liffey Press, Dublin 2007; Areopagita Publishing 2017). *The Welkinn Complex* (Number One Son, Florida, FL., 2011; Revised Edition Amazon 2015). *SOS Lusitania* 2012 (O'Brien Press, 2012) which was the 'One Book One Community' in the Lusitania Centenary year of 2015. *UCD Belfield Metaphysical: A Retrospective* (Lapwing Press, Belfast 2017). Plays broadcast on RTÉ: *Children of No Importance* and *Multiple Indiscretions*. *In this Supreme Hour* The Playhouse, Derry 2016. *UCD Belfield Metaphysical: New and Selected Poems* (Areopagitica Publishing 2018). *Harvard's Patron: Jack of All Poets* (Areopagitica Publishing, 2018).

Selected Anthology Listings: *Something Sensational To Read in the Train* anthology foreword: Brendan Kennelly (Lemon Soap Press, Dublin 2005); *Catullus: One Man of Verona* anthology ed. Ronan Sheehan (Farmar & Farmar Ltd., 2010); *Ends & Beginnings* anthology eds John Gery and William Pratt (AMS Press Inc., New York 2011); *A Map of Melancholy* (long poem) in *Windows Anthology* eds. Heather Brett and Noel Monahan 2012; *In Place of Love and Country* eds. Richard Parker & John Gery (Crater Press, London 2013); *Liberty, Come Galloping! Salvation, Flower: Poets Worldwide Anthology* ed. Kamran Mir Hazar (Kabul Press 2013); *Still Anthology* ed. Chelley McLear (CAP, Belfast 2014); *Where Two Rivers Meet* ed. Kevin Kiely, Artskills NI 2015; *West Side Stories* ed. Kevin Kiely Eden Place Arts Centre, Derry NI 2015; *Cork Literary Review Anthology* ed. Kathy D'Arcy (Bradshaw Books, 2016); *1916-2016: An Anthology of Reactions* eds. John Liddy and Dominic Taylor (Limerick Arts Centre, 2016).

CPSIA information can be obtained
at www.ICGtesting.com
Printed in the USA
LVHW050101250119
605231LV00006B/135/P